SOLOMON'S MEMORY PALACE

A Freemason's Guide to the Ancient Art of Memoria Verborum

BOB W. LINGERFELT

COVER

An emblem from Achille Bocchi's (1488-1562) "Symbolicarum Quaestionum." Above this emblem, in the book, appear the words "PICTURIA GRAVIUM OSTENDUNTUR PONDERA RERUM. QUAEQUE LATENT IMACES, HAEC PER MAGE APERTA PATENT," *which loosely translates as, "A picture illustrates the deep insights of important matters; whatever is unseen can be made visible."*

Solomon's Memory Palace
A Freemason's Guide to *Memoria Verborum*
By Bob W. Lingerfelt
1927LA@gmail.com

Motey Publishing, Omaha, Nebraska

Copyright Bob W. Lingerfelt

All rights reserved. No part of this book may be reproduced in any form or by any electronic or mechanical means, including information storage and retrieval systems, without written permission from the publisher or author, except in the case of a reviewer, who may quote brief passages embodied in critical articles or in a review.

I welcome feedback on how to make this book better. Please contact me at 1927LA@gmail.com.

If you found this book useful, a positive review would be very much appreciated.

❋ Created with Vellum

* * *

"...an excellent beginner's guide. Lingerfelt does a good job of keeping it simple...If your goal is to improve in Masonic knowledge and Freemasonry in general, this book is a useful addition to your own Masonic education, and when you're done with it, it makes an excellent gift for your first student."

- Sir Knight Michael F. Feld, *Knights Templar,* Volume LXV, Number 6, June 2019

*Dedicated to my brothers,
the builders and keepers of secrets*

CONTENTS

Preface	xiii
1. The Importance of Memory in the Craft	1
2. The Challenge of Masonic Memorization	5
3. A Solution for Freemasons	9
4. Some Words of Encouragement	16
5. Types of Memorization	20
6. Architecture	27
7. Memory Objects	34
8. The Qualities of Memory Objects	38
9. How to Create Memory Objects	47
10. The Model	62
11. Spaces	76
12. Areas	80
13. Focal Points	83
14. The Human Body	92
15. The Eye	99
16. Traveling	102
17. Establishing Landmarks	113
18. Planning Your Memory Palace	117
19. Motion and Interaction as Cement	123
20. Memory Palace Example	126
21. Process Overview	135
22. The Power of Omission	138
23. Compartmentalization	141
24. Best Practices	143
25. Maintenance	156
26. Supplementary Techniques	159
27. Some Closing Thoughts	168

Finale	179
Appendix 1: Memory Object Samples	183
Appendix 2: Archaic Words Explained	191
Appendix 3: Notations	197
Also by Bob W. Lingerfelt	205

By associating ideas with things, a grand mnemonic system is established and their perpetuity provided for. Tablets may be shattered, lettered obelisks be upturned, parchments rot, libraries perish, but truth, bound to nature, can never perish until her funeral pyre is lighted by the torch of doom. So, poets and artists, by their idealizations, impress material objects with an inner glory and a hidden life...Our ethical system is a long-drawn corridor of pictured truths.

- Br. Howard Henderson, *Autumn Leaves Gathered in Indian Summer* (1907)

PREFACE

It is difficult not to feel a little like an imposter when writing about memory palaces, or more specifically, memory palaces used for the purpose of *memoria verborum* (memory of words). The art of building memory palaces has been taught for more than two millennia and many books have been written about the subject by far more important and learned people than me; people who merit entries in encyclopedias and history books or who have an extraordinary number of letters and dots after their names.

Yet the overwhelming majority of these books focus not on *memoria verborum* but its simpler counterpart *memoria rerum* (memory of things). Additionally, most books about the art of memory are historical overviews or comparative studies. Few teach, much less advocate, its actual practice. I'm not aware of single modern text that teaches *memoria verborum* using the memory palace technique.

There is also a curious absence of memory books of any kind written for Freemasons or which explore the ties between our craft's rites and the art of memory. This has always seemed peculiar to me, given the unique memorization restrictions imposed on Masons, the pressing needs of our fraternity, and the great number of books available on Freemasonry in general.

That said, this book is not reserved for Freemasons. True, there are allusions here and there to certain Masonic concepts and practices, but a knowledge of Freemasonry is not needed to grasp the fundamentals. Anyone interested in the rarely taught *memoria verborum* memory palace technique will hopefully find this book useful.

- Bob W. Lingerfelt, P.M.
Education Committee, Grand Lodge of Nebraska A.F.&A.M.
Bellevue Lodge #325, Nebraska
Saints John Lodge of Education #331
Tabula Rasa Lodge #332, Nebraska
Scottish Rite, Omaha Valley
S.R.I.C.F.

THE IMPORTANCE OF MEMORY IN THE CRAFT

While non-Masons interested in memorization techniques should find *Solomon's Memory Palace* very useful, I have written it primarily for Freemasons who are looking for a better way to memorize Masonic materials. In the pages that follow I will teach you a special and rare version of the *method of loci*, an ancient approach to memorization which has cryptic ties to the establishment of the Speculative Freemasonry in the 17th and 18th centuries.

Memory, the ability to store and recall information, plays a critical role in Freemasonry. In many ways, it is at the very heart of Masonry. What would be the utility of all our emblems, symbols, hieroglyphs, and signs if we could not remember their purpose? What point would there be in gathering as a lodge if no one present had taken the time to memorize the rituals, lectures, or floor-work? What would be the criteria for a Mason to pass from one degree to another? How would we decipher the esoteric words?

Memory grants us wisdom, and without wisdom, a lodge cannot be supported. Without memory to connect us to our past, we cannot make Masons. Without memory, we cannot prudentially determine the outcomes of our present and future actions, and without Prudence, the virtues of Temperance, Fortitude, and Justice are blind. We can't temper our actions without knowing what is wrong or right; we won't endure pain, peril, or danger without first knowing that our cause is worth fighting for; we can't have a standard of justice without first knowing what is fair and equitable.

Masonic emblems exist to remind us of specific principles, concepts, mysteries, and truths. Yet they only serve their purpose if we, as members of the craft, remember what they represent. And what would happen to those secrets which we have sworn never to write or otherwise physically record, and which have been passed brother to brother, in secret, for centuries? What would happen to those secrets that defy words, which only our minds can host in full?

Many brothers might be unaware that William Schaw, a pivotal figure in the history of Freemasonry, prohibited the admittance of anyone into a lodge who could not demonstrate skill in "the art of memory." In 1599, he ordered the General Warden to "test every fellow of the craft and every apprentice on the art of memory and science thereof," adding that, "fellows of craft…shall not be admitted without a sufficient test and proof of memory and art of craft."

Almost four centuries later, author and historian Frances A. Yates, in her book *The Art of Memory*, suggested that Speculative Freemasonry might owe a debt to Renaissance practitioners of the art of memory, writing, "The origins of Freemasonry are wrapped in mystery...I would think that the answer to this problem may be suggested by the history of the art of memory...which used, not the real architecture of 'operative' masonry, but the imaginary or 'speculative' architecture of the art of memory as the vehicle of its teachings."

Yates' speculation is worthy of contemplation. Most practitioners of the art of memory in the sixteenth and seventeenth centuries used some form of the memory palace technique taught in this book, and many of those practitioners can be connected to individuals identified with nescient Speculative Freemasonry.

In fact, the tools of Freemasonry and the tools used to "erect" a memory palace are strikingly similar. Both use structures – a temple and palace, respectively – as foundational structures or frameworks. Both communicate via myriad symbols, emblems, and hieroglyphs. Both require the practitioner to perform a type of mental navigation using symbols as waypoints. Both use the five senses as gateways between the physical and the mental worlds. Both draw designs on blank canvases (which can be thought of as tracing boards). Both make use of one-, two-, and three-dimensional geometric figures, to include points, lines, planes, cubes, and cylinders.

As to why the art of memory might have been realized and perpetuated by Speculative Freemasonry, one needs to delve into the teachings of Renaissance scholars such as Giulio Camillo (c.1480-1544), John Dee (1527-1608), Giordano Bruno (1548-1600), Alexander Dickson (c.1558-1604), and Robert Fludd (1574-1637). These men believed that a memory palace could do more than just improve a person's memory.

They believed that, properly constructed, a memory palace could provide its creator with divine insight - often referred to as "light."

If this topic interests you, there are a number of books that address it with varying levels of detail. Two that are on my bookshelf are David Stevenson's *The Origins of Freemasonry* and Robert Cooper's *Cracking the Freemason's Code*. Frances Yates's *The Art of Memory*, previously mentioned, is not a book about Freemasonry per se but is perhaps the greatest book yet written about the art of memory and memory palaces, and in it, Yates discusses the potential ties between the art and the fraternity. Paolo Rossi's *Logic and the Art of Memory* doesn't mention Freemasonry even once, yet Freemasons should find several items of interest within its pages.

But let's not go too far afield. You're likely reading this book because you simply want an effective way to memorize some part of our ritual, and for that, I thank you. You have taken a step that many brothers will never take.

For many Freemasons, memorization of craft materials is perceived as a burdensome additional duty that has little or no value. Yet memorization is fundamental to our craft. If new Masons are unwilling to memorize rituals, roles, and lectures, our fraternity will die - and soon. Saying that there is too much memory work in Freemasonry is like saying there is too much running back and forth in football. You simply can't have one without the other.

Fortunately, the memory palace provides all of us a place to safely store those ancient treasures so important to our order.

Unfortunately, they don't build themselves.

Let's get to work.

2
THE CHALLENGE OF MASONIC MEMORIZATION

I will soar, then, beyond this power of my nature also, still rising by degrees toward him who made me. And I enter the fields and spacious halls of memory, where are stored as treasures the countless images that have been brought into them from all manner of things by the senses. There, in the memory, is likewise stored what we cogitate, either by enlarging or reducing our perceptions, or by altering one way or another those things which the senses have made contact with; and everything else that has been entrusted to it and stored up in it, which oblivion has not yet swallowed up and buried.

- Augustine of Hippo (354-430), *The Confessions* (c.398)

Do you struggle to memorize roles, charges, lectures, or other parts of ritual? If so, you may have decided that your brain simply isn't wired for that kind of thing, which means you've probably stopped trying. Why fight nature, right?

But your brain probably isn't the problem. The real problem may be your technique - or lack of technique. Your brain is a tool, just like a hammer. A hammer has to be used correctly to be effective. Using a hammer's claw to drive a nail into a piece of wood is bad technique. So is using the handle to try to remove a nail. In both cases you've got the perfect tool for the job but you're using it the wrong way.

Ironically, while you spent years in school being tested on your ability to memorize what you were taught, the one thing you were probably never taught is how to memorize things. In hindsight, that seems a bit unfair, doesn't it? Shouldn't that have been the *first* thing you were taught?

Now that you're an adult, you're on your own. Sure, there are plenty of books, websites, and videos that promise to teach you the secrets of memorization. Some of them are quite good. However, most are designed for students, motivational speakers, business professionals, politicians, clergy, educators, and, of course, actors.

That's a problem because those individuals have different needs than you and operate with fewer restrictions. Your objective is to recite your material verbatim, i.e., word-for-word, while most others, excluding actors, only need to memorize the outline of what they plan to say. The "scripts" of motivational speakers and college lecturers, for example, are flexible. The individuals who use them need only to move from one major topic to another in a logical fashion, and to address the most important aspects of each topic. Also, they can refer to notes while speaking – a luxury you do not have in lodge.

Actors are held to a higher standard. In most cases, actors are supposed to remember their lines verbatim. Shakespearean actors, in particular, face many of the same challenges as Freemasons. They must memorize words that are rarely if ever used in modern society and which are strung together in sentences that are difficult to comprehend. The amount of material that must be memorized is staggering. An actor portraying Hamlet must memorize more than 1,500 lines! Like Freemasons, actors – or, at least, stage actors – cannot rely on notes or teleprompters during a performance.

Nevertheless, even Shakespearean actors have several advantages over Freemasons. Masons are prohibited from writing or recording any of the esoteric portions of a lecture or part, even for personal use. Masons are not permitted to rehearse with a non-Mason or a Mason not of the appropriate degree, and there are some things that cannot be said aloud outside of lodge. There are no video or audio recordings of lectures that Masons can watch in their homes or listen to while traveling. Worse, Masonic "scripts" are often in code.

Most Shakespearean actors would balk if told that their scripts would be in code; that some of the words would be omitted from the script altogether; that they could only rehearse their lines on stage, and only with another actor (and even then, only with *certain* actors); and that they were prohibited from ever writing or recording their lines, or saying them aloud outside the theater, or in front of any non-actors, or in any environment where they might be overheard.

Another thing that distinguishes what Freemasons memorize from those things memorized by a motivational speaker, politician, instructor, or actor is *purpose*. Outside of Freemasonry, lecturers seek to educate or inform. Actors and singers seek to entertain. Politicians seek to persuade or motivate. Their words are intended for others, and without an audience, they aren't spoken.

In Freemasonry, what we memorize and recite is *ritual*. It is the very "stuff" of the craft, required even when there is almost no one there to hear it (or no one listening). Yet the words must be said correctly. Yes, what is memorized and recited also serves to educate candidates and brothers, but if education was the only purpose we would not be required to remember our words verbatim.

This is why so many memory books and videos available to the public simply don't work for Freemasons. They are written for individuals who have far more liberties than Freemasons do and they advise us to do things we have sworn not to do.

3
A SOLUTION FOR FREEMASONS

Luckily, *some* of the memorization techniques used by the world at large are usable by Freemasons. Among the most effective of these is the memory palace, also known as the *method of loci*. This is an ancient technique which, as mentioned earlier, may be historically tied to Freemasonry, making it both effective and appropriate.

One of the earliest descriptions of a memory palace can be found in a book called *Rhetorica Ad Herennium*, which is Latin for *Rhetoric: For Herennius*.

Rhetoric refers to persuasive or effective speaking, and the book was actually written for a gentleman named Gaius Herennius, whom we know nothing about. To be honest, we don't even know who wrote the book. It was attributed to Cicero (106 B.C.- 43 B.C.) for a long time but the consensus today is that he was not the author. We do know it was written about 80 B.C.

If you already find this topic a bit daunting, it's only

because there's so much Latin been thrown around. Essentially some guy in a toga (let's call him Carl) wrote a book called "A Guide to Effective Speaking" and dedicated to another guy in a toga (let's call him Harry). Maybe Harry was a lawyer who'd lost a few too many cases, or a politician who wasn't very popular with his peers or those he represented.

In any event, the book that Carl wrote for Harry was a good one, and it was copied again and again, and because it was so good and so many copies were made, it has survived twenty-one hundred years and is still with us. So, the next time you see *Ad Herennium* (the shortened title of *Rhetorica Ad Herennium*), just think of it as Public Speaking for Harry. That's a lot less intimidating, isn't it?

Carl's book, dedicated to Harry, is the oldest surviving book which describes how a memory palace is built and used, which means it has been referenced by almost every other writer on the topic since then, to include me – and I'll be referring to it a lot.

But let's get back to the basics. What, exactly, is a memory palace?

It's easier to demonstrate than to explain. Here's a very basic example:

Imagine that you are in a room. Any room. In your home, for example. Just choose a room at random. Got it? Okay, now imagine there is a giant, bloodshot eye painted on one of the walls.

That's weird, huh? Why the heck would anyone paint a giant, bloodshot eye on your wall?

Now, picture yourself walking from that room to an adjacent room. Imagine that in the adjacent room there is a metal can. Any kind of can. A paint can, or a can of beans. It can be on the floor, or on a piece of furniture, or dangling from the ceiling by a piece of string. Whatever you want.

Easy, right?

So, in one room you have a giant bloodshot eye, and in the next room, you have a can. Go back to the room with the eye painted on the wall, and say aloud what you see. "Eye."

Now mentally "walk" to the next room and say aloud what you see there. "Can."

Eye - Can.

Or, in plain English, "I can."

There you go. You just created a memory palace.

※

YOU MAY BE THINKING THAT THE "EYE - CAN" EXAMPLE IS silly. You don't need an ancient memorization system to remember a two-word sentence. Can such a simple system really be used to memorize a thousand-word lecture?

Absolutely. I speak from experience. Using this system, only six months after becoming a Mason, I was giving the third section lectures for both the Entered Apprentice's and Master Mason's degree. I memorized these parts by devoting just a few hours each week to building memory palaces.

I am not a rocket scientist. Nor was I experienced in the memory palace technique. Prior to learning how to use a memory palace, I found even the abridged proficiency tests for the degrees challenging.

Of course, the real authorities on the effectiveness of memory palaces are those researchers and practitioners who have made the brain, memory, and memorization their life's work. What do they have to say?

Let's start with the hardcore practitioners. Do you know what a *brain athlete* is? It's a person who matches his or her memory against the memories of hundreds of others in competitions around the world. Perhaps you've seen their exploits on television or the internet. Shuffle twenty-seven decks of playing cards together and hand the new giant stack to one of these individuals and they'll be able to memorize the ranks and suits of every card in sequence in less than an hour. Given thirty minutes, some of them can memorize a string of four thousand numbers.

An excellent overview of these athletes and the competitive world they live in is captured in Joshua Foer's fun and accessible best-seller, *Moonwalking with Einstein: The Art and Science of Remembering Everything*. The bottom line is that these are people who take memorization very, very seriously.

What's their secret? You guessed it. The memory palace.

Per the *New Scientist* article, *How to Train Your Brain to Be Like a Memory Champion's*:

> The strategy almost all top memorisers rely on is the 'method of loci', which involves imagining a route that they know well, such as moving around their home or traveling to work, and associating the information to be learned with landmarks along that route. They can then retrieve the information later on by making the same journey in their mind and seeing the objects connected to each landmark.

As I mentioned earlier, *method of loci* is the ancient name for the memory palace technique. More on that later.

AT THIS POINT YOU MIGHT OBJECT THAT YOU ARE NOT A brain athlete. No problem. You don't need to be. The memory palace technique can be learned by anyone. Recent studies have shown that just six weeks of memory palace study can give the average person a superior memory.

One study conducted at Radboud University, in the Netherlands, found that brain athletes' brains (specifically, those who used memory palaces) are anatomically like any other brains, but operate differently. In a sense, the memory palace experts are using the same computer as the rest of us but with a different operating system. More intriguingly, the memory palace brains continue to operate differently even when they *aren't* trying to memorize something. Such brains appear to have been completely reprogrammed.

Surprised at this finding, researchers brought in a group test subjects (none of them brain athletes) and scanned their brains. The results were unexceptional. Then they taught them how to use the memory palace and scanned their brains again. Amazingly, the brains of the test subjects began to operate just like those of the brain athletes – even when they weren't trying to remember anything! Just like the brain athletes, the test subjects' brains seemed to have been reprogrammed simply by the exercise of building memory palaces.

And they had developed excellent memories. As reported by *New Scientist*:

> After just six weeks' training, participants more than doubled their performance in a memory test, and scans showed their brains were functioning more like those of competitive memorisers.

Memory palaces take maximum advantage how our brains work. The creation and population of memory palaces relies on a part of the brain called the *hippocampus*, which has some very peculiar and useful abilities.

First, it is the seat of spatial awareness, or the ability to remember how to get from one place to another, use landmarks to determine where you are, and calculate the distances between locations. It also establishes relationships between space and time. These skills are critical for human survival.

Second, hippocampus consolidates short-term and long-term memory.

Third, the hippocampus is one of those magical regions of the brain where new neurons are created, a process referred to as *neurogenesis*, which may play a role in learning and memorization.

The brain's neural networks are flexible. Memorization through memory palaces opens up new neural pathways, and once the brain is introduced to those paths, it continues to use them *even when a person isn't building a memory palace*. This results in major and long-lasting changes to how your brain works, which can lead to superior memory performance.

The studies done at Radboud University and other institutions also demonstrated that memorization done the old-fashioned way - pounding things into your head by repetition – has no lasting benefit. Your brain never learns new paths, and while you may eventually memorize whatever you're studying, your ability to memorize other things will not improve.

So, there you go. It appears the ancient builders of mind palaces intuitively knew something we have only recently rediscovered through scientific studies and the exploits of brain athletes: If you want a superior memory and weren't gifted with one, *you can build one.*

❧ 4 ☙
SOME WORDS OF ENCOURAGEMENT

Thumbing through this book, you're going to encounter a lot of scary-looking things: Latin, dates, weirdly long and unpronounceable names, charts, lists, and diagrams. There's even an appendix! Nothing with an *appendix* can be user-friendly, can it?!

Don't panic. It's not nearly as bad as it looks. Here are some things you should know, and a few pieces of advice:

- This is not a textbook. The basics of building a memory palace are very simple, and the basics are all you need to get the job done. I've included a lot of information in this book that goes beyond the basics, but most of the information is for reference purposes only. Don't let the extra stuff intimidate you. You don't really need to know the difference between a homonym, a homophone, and a homograph, or the difference between an emblem and a symbol. It doesn't matter if you use the term "Memory Objects" or "images" or "shadows" or "lookedy-look-looks."

- There is no perfect way to construct a memory palace. Of the information I provide, use only what you need. If you want to do something other than what I suggest, go for it. If you come up with a better idea, use it. If something confuses you, skip it. I've read many books and articles on memory palaces and I don't follow any of them to the letter. Like you will do, I took the bits and pieces that appealed to me and hobbled them together in a way that best suited how my brain works.
- Memorize at your own pace. Set your own schedule. If you can memorize a sentence a day, that's fine. If you only have time for few words a day, that's fine also. Maybe you'll memorize a lecture in a month. Maybe it will take a year. Maybe it will take two years. Even two years is better than never, right? If you ever feel like you've bitten off more than you can chew, slow down. Take smaller bites. But keep chewing.
- Don't give up. Never forget that you are helping your lodge as much as you are helping yourself. You are, in fact, helping preserve the entire fraternity. You will become a contributor and participant instead of a spectator.
- In memorizing rites, parts, and lectures you will obtain an intimate knowledge of what is contained in them. Listening to a lecture and studying a lecture for purposes of memorization and recital

are very different things. Memorization requires you to focus on every word. You are almost certain to make many discoveries through memorization that you would have never made simply listening to others.
- Creating memory palaces literally changes how your brain works, and in a good way. Learning how to create memory palaces may provide you with the skills and insight needed to create other mental "palaces" beneficial to you as a Freemason.
- The rites, parts, lectures, etc., of Freemasonry are difficult not only because of their length but because of the way the sentences are formed. The language is archaic. The order of the words seems unnatural – even nonsensical - to many modern readers. It's a lot like reading Shakespeare, but in code. It's no wonder that so many Masons shy away from memorization. The memory palace technique overcomes these issues by transforming the words into objects of your choosing. Remembering these objects in the correct order is easier than remembering the words in the right order, and the objects will help you pronounce the words correctly.
- Lastly, but perhaps most importantly for a few of you in the craft: a person who builds memory palaces, and populates them with memory objects, is doing more than just improving his memory. He is inadvertently learning how to recognize, navigate, and deconstruct, or reverse-engineer, the memory palaces carefully crafted by others in

previous centuries and concealed in the writings and illustrations of some of our greatest thinkers. If you're a traveller, certain waypoints that were invisible will become visible, and following them may lead you to new and exciting places.

❧ 5 ❧
TYPES OF MEMORIZATION

The student wishing to acquire 'memory for words' begins in the same way as the 'memory for things' student; that is to say he memorizes places which are to hold his images. But he is confronted with a harder task for far more places will be needed to memorize all the words of a speech than would be needed for its notions.

- Frances Yates, *The Art of Memory*

The building of memory palaces to retain memories is an ancient practice that pre-dates the birth of Christ and which has undergone centuries of refinement, neglect, ridicule, and praise. It is one of many methods that have been taught to increase *artificial* memory, which is simply memory improved by training. The numerous methods to enhance artificial memory are collectively known as the *art of memory*, though this might be more clearly understood as the *art of memorization*.

Memory palaces are generally used for one of two purposes:

1. To help you remember a list of distinct items, often in a prescribed sequence
2. To help you remember long written passages verbatim (word-for-word).

These are commonly known as *memoria rerum* (memory of things) and *memoria verborum* (memory of words).

These terms are Latin because our oldest records of the techniques are in Latin and scholars since then have continued to use them. Improvement of the memory has long been considered more art than science. Many of the most authoritative texts on the subject were written centuries ago by theologians, philosophers, scientists, and mystics, each promoting their own interpretations, agendas, and techniques. The earliest manuals and commentaries were written in Greek and Latin. Later additions were made in Italian, Spanish, French, and English.

In this book, I've attempted to reconcile, digest, and reintroduce these varied sources in such a way that they are accessible to the modern reader, and, of equal importance, useful to the modern ritualists in our ancient fraternity. For that reason, some of the methods and terms I use in this book will not be found in other sources - at least not explicitly. I've distilled certain complicated concepts down to the essentials. Whenever possible I use plain English in lieu of archaic or foreign words.

In keeping with that policy, I will be referring to *memoria rerum* as "list memorization" and *memoria verborum* as "verbatim memorization." These are explained below.

LIST MEMORIZATION (MEMORIA RERUM)

List Memorization is the primary system used by competitive brain athletes. It is used to remember a list of items, facts, numbers, or talking points, usually in a specific order. Things you might memorize using this system are a shopping list, a long string of numbers, the names of states, or the order of playing cards in a deck.

List memorization was favored for thousands of years by politicians, orators, lecturers, and lawyers because it can be used to memorize a list of topics which an individual wishes to speak about, as well as the sequence in which the topics are to be presented. These individuals do not need to write a speech and memorize it word-for-word. A politician, for example, might want to discuss the following topics with his constituents:

- taxes
- immigration
- organized labor
- natural disasters
- war

His polling data shows that voters are most concerned about taxes, so it's important he discuss those first. The other topics are listed in descending order of importance, with war being, for now, the least important issue, so he plans on touching on that topic only briefly toward the close of his speech. In preparation for this speech he constructs a simple five-room memory palace. Room one contains a pile of money; room two, a barbed wire fence; room three, a union member with a picket sign; room four, a fire; and room five, a soldier.

True, he could avoid the use of a memory placing by simply referring to index cards while speaking. Card one might read, "Taxes," card two "Immigration," etc. Or he could refer to a bullet list he's stored on his smart phone. But today, as in the past, politicians and other public speakers avoid the use of reference materials when speaking in public. They want to appear smart and confident, and they want to maintain eye contract with their listeners. Continually glancing at a smart phone or fumbling with index cards or a written script destroys the hypnotic connection between speaker and listener. That's why today's high-ranking officials use teleprompters and ear pieces, which, like memory palaces, are invisible to audiences.

In fact, this is why our old friend "Carl" included a section on memory in *Ad Herennium*. Remember, the book was about persuasive speaking, not memory. Most of the book has nothing to do with memory. But then, as today, a public speaker was a lot less persuasive if he broke eye contact with his audience to refer to his notes.

VERBATIM MEMORIZATION (MEMORIA VERBORUM)

Verbatim Memorization, or memory of words, is used to memorize a speech, role, lecture, etc., word-for word. It is a happy coincidence that "verbatim" is a Latin word still used and understood by English speakers today. Verbatim memorization obviously requires much more effort than list memorization because you'll need to create a lot more Spaces and Memory Objects. Instead of remembering just a list of items, you're attempting to memorize entire paragraphs – entire pages, in fact. Word-for-word.

The following scenarios should help you understand the difference between list and verbatim memorization techniques.

Imagine a school in which a science teacher, Mrs. Baker, has instructed her students to remember the names of all the planets in our solar system, the planets' distances from the sun, and the number and names of each their moons. This is no easy task. Saturn alone has over fifty moons!

Luckily for the students, Mrs. Baker has taught them how to build memory palaces using the list memorization technique. Each student dutifully uses the technique to memorize all the information required, placing each planet in a specific room of his or her memory palace and then carefully placing the corresponding moons into corners, atop furniture, inside lamps, etc..

A week later, Mrs. Baker asks several students to stand up in class and name the moons of Saturn. To her joy, they all answer correctly. Yet they do *not* all say the same thing. One student might identify Saturn's moons in alphabetical order. The second might identify them in order of their proximity to Saturn. The third, from largest to smallest. Even if all of the students memorized the moons in the same order, they'd still use their own words to describe that order. One might say,

"The nearest moon to Saturn is Minas..." while another could say, "The moon closest to Saturn is called Minas..." and so on. The *exact words* don't matter, so long as the *list* is correct.

In this situation, list memorization has served the students well.

But, next door, Mr. Smith, an American History teacher, has tasked *his* students to memorize the Gettysburg Address. His students don't have the luxury of Mrs. Baker's students. They have no wiggle room. Every student will need to memorize every word of Lincoln's speech *in the exact order in which Lincoln spoke them*. If asked to recite the speech in class, every student will be expected to say exactly same thing.

In this scenario, list memorization won't get the job done. What Mr. Smith's students need is verbatim memorization.

GOING FORWARD

The rest of this book is dedicated to teaching you how to build a memory palace that can be used for verbatim memorization. Because this approach is simply list memorization taken to a much higher level, you'll actually be learning both methods at once. Which you elect to use depends on your needs, abilities and preferences. If you are good at memorizing sentences or even paragraphs, and you simply need a way to organize your thoughts, list memorization may be sufficient. In such cases all you really need is a series of Memory Objects that will remind you of the content of each paragraph and its place in the proper order of things.

If you need help memorizing the words themselves, you'll want to use the verbatim approach. It requires the creation of a Memory Object for every word, or cluster of words. It is thus more complex and requires much more time than list memorization.

6
ARCHITECTURE

"The artificial memory includes backgrounds and images. By backgrounds I mean such scenes as are naturally or artificially set off on a small scale, complete and conspicuous, so that we can grasp and embrace them easily by the natural memory."

- *Ad Herennium*

There are two primary components to a memory palace:

THE MODEL

The model is a mental image of a real-world location, such as your house, school, grocery store, etc. The Model's purpose is to provide structure and organize your Memory Objects, discussed next. It ensures that you'll memorize and recite the words in the correct order. Historically, these have been referred to as *loci*, which is Latin for *places*. That is why the memory palace technique is often referred to as the *Method of Loci*, i.e., the Location Method. Masonically, a Model is analogous to a blank tracing board, and your Memory Objects are analogous to the emblems or symbols drawn or painted on that tracing board. Memory palaces are very much like tracing boards, except that they exist only in your mind, and are three-dimensional. Alternatively, you can think of your Model as a journal of blank pages, and the Memory Objects as drawings you'll be making in that journal.

MEMORY OBJECTS

Memory Objects are mental visions of objects that remind you of concepts or words you need to memorize. In other books, old and new, these might be referred to as *mnemonics, mnemonic objects, adjects,* or *imagines*.

Mnemonic is an old Greek word which can be either an adjective ("pertaining to memory") or a noun ("a thing that assists the memory"). The *m* before the *n* is silent. I won't be using that term because I think it causes English readers to stumble. There's something unnatural about starting any word with *mn* and it can be very distracting. My apologies to the purists.

Imagines means "imagined things" or "mental pictures." Today, this term is most often translated into English as *image*. I don't like the term *image* because it implies a two-dimensional thing which is "seen" by the mind's eye, like a painting or photograph. But the things used to remember words are best imagined as three-dimensional. *Imagined things* is better, but your Model, described below, is also imagined (though typically an imagined version of a real place). We need a term this distinguishes the Model from the things used to remember words. So, in this book, we'll use the term *Memory Object*.

You might wonder why you should bother memorizing two sets of things (Memory Objects and their related words) instead of just one set of things (the words). Isn't that inefficient? Aren't you basically doubling the amount of stuff you need to memorize? Why not just do things the old-fashioned way and read, read, and re-read all your material until it gets pounded into your head? Isn't that what you did in school? Didn't that work well enough?

It's a good question. In fact, critics of the verbatim form of the memory palace have leveled that accusation against the technique for thousands of years. Even the Roman rhetorician Quintilian (c. 35 – c. 100 AD), one of the most famous proponents of the system as a basic memory device, thought it useless for remembering long passages. He wrote, "It [the memory palace] will however be of less service in retaining the parts of a speech...how can such an art grasp a whole series of connected words...will not the flow of our speech inevitably be impeded by the double task imposed on our memory? For how can our words be expected to flow in connected speech, if we have to look back at separate forms for each individual word?"

Even those who acknowledge that the technique is effective often wonder aloud whether the effort of building a memory palace is worth the reward.

Frances Yates wrote "There is no doubt that this method will work for anyone who is prepared to labour seriously at these mnemonic gymnastics," yet admitting, "I have never attempted to do so myself..." Though concluding that "the system evidently worked," author David Stevenson noted that, "A first reaction to the art of memory is likely to be that it would surely hinder rather than help the unfortunate orator..." And author Robert Cooper writes that "the amount of material that has come down to us from the Roman period shows that the technique worked well and was widely used..." yet, "In today's world we may think this technique strange, even absurd..."

To be fair, most historians who write about memory palaces are not practitioners. They do not pretend to be. Their books provide valuable insight into the history of memory palaces and the art of memory in general, and for that we are indebted to them. They are fantastic books I'd recommend to anyone. But they are histories, not self-help books.

Let me clear up a few misconceptions some people (not necessarily these authors) have about using memory palaces for verbatim memorization.

The first is that, during recitation, a practitioner must first think of the Memory Object and then wait for the corresponding word to come to him, which results in a slow, laborious, and at times, awkward, recitation.

The second is that a Memory Object used to memorize a word must be forever remembered. This would mean that if you forget a Memory Object you'll also forget the word or words associated with it.

If these two objections were valid, I'd agree that a memory palace is not suited for verbatim memorization. Fortunately, they are not accurate. You don't, in fact, need to remember the Memory Objects you used to build your memory palace -

not for long, anyway. In fact, you may forget them even before you stand up in lodge and recite what you've memorized.

Memory Objects are temporary. They are like molds used to impress the correct words into your brain when you first endeavor to memorize a passage. Think of them like braces on crooked teeth, or a cast on a broken arm, or training wheels on child's bicycle. The Memory Objects mold your memory in much the same way. They are not intended to be permanent. They'll remain in your memory for a few hours, days, weeks, or months, before eventually receding into the background.

But the words will remain.

The author of *Ad Herennium* seems to have understood this, writing, "...such an arrangement of images succeeds only if we use our notation to stimulate the natural memory, so that we first go over a given verse twice or three times to ourselves and then represent the words by means of images. In this way art will supplement nature. For neither by itself will be strong enough..."

Are the Memory Objects forever lost once the words have taken root in our brains? Are the molds broken and discarded? I don't know. I can recall fewer than 5% of the Memory Objects I used to memorize lectures, yet I feel they are still there, like ghosts, in some part of my mind. Perhaps they are still anchoring my words in place, unseen. Perhaps they have sunk into my subconscious but are still performing some purpose. What I can say, with confidence, is that I rarely summon Memory Objects for any words in those lectures I've known for more than a month. The words come automatically.

If this surprises you, consider that, as children, we learn

each letter of the alphabet and its pronunciation, and when we read elementary texts we take great care to pronounce each letter of a word. It's not until we pronounce the last letter of a written word that we know what the word is, and what it alludes to.

Yet as adults, we grasp what is written by merely scanning the words on a computer screen or piece of paper, paying no attention to the individual letters or how they are pronounced. Does this mean it was pointless for us to learn the pronunciation of the letters and words as children? Of course not. That was a necessary stage in the learning process. That we don't read today as we were initially taught to read is irrelevant. One phase naturally preceded the other.

Memory Objects work in a similar manner. We use them to deeply impress words into our brains, in the proper order. When that is done, the Memory Objects can be discarded.

The Model, however, will remain in place, and the words will remain attached to it. Put another way, though the Memory Objects tend to evaporate over time, you'll find that the words you've memorized remain associated with specific locations within your Model. Consequently, you may still find your mind wandering your old memory palace while reciting some part that you've memorized even if the Memory Objects are gone. Your mind's eye will focus on the former location of that Memory Object, and the location can, by itself, trigger the word. In this curious way, the Focus Points later discussed take the place of the Memory Objects, and ultimately serve the same purpose.

Another objection made by non-practitioners is that the use of memory palaces for verbatim memorization somehow prevents a student from grasping the meaning of what is being memorized. This objection assumes the jumble of Memory Objects in a person's head allows him to remember the required words without actually comprehending what he is talking about.

Yet this same argument could be made against rote memory, i.e., memorizing words, sentences, and paragraphs the old-fashioned way - reading and repeating, reading and repeating, until the words stick. It is easy for a person to regurgitate words memorized through rote efforts without comprehending what the words mean, as a whole.

The memory palace at least requires you to think about the words you're memorizing and how they connect to one another. Rote memorization merely requires that you be able to parrot them.

7
MEMORY OBJECTS

Everything that strikes the eye more immediately engages the attention, and imprints on the memory serious and solemn truths.
 - William Preston, *Illustrations of Masonry* (1775)

A Memory Object is a thing or group of things that you create with your imagination and then place in a specific location in your memory palace to remind you of a word or words.

"Thing" has a very broad meaning when applied to Memory Objects. Things include people, objects, animals, sunlight, lightning, shadows, mist, plants, colors, and much more. If you can see, feel, touch, taste, or hear it, whatever "it" is, that thing can be used as a Memory Object, or as a component of a Memory Object.

If you were trying to memorize the phrase, "Amiable Conduct, " your Memory Object could be a convict in a striped prisoner's uniform. He stands facing you, his arms raised in the air, as if surrendering. In his right hand, he holds a rifle with a powerful scope. In his left hand, he holds a duck. His head isn't a normal head – in fact, it's the head of a bull! For some reason, a giant "E" has been stitched on to the front of his uniform. Maybe his name is Ed?

Moving clockwise in your mind's eye, you see this: a rifle with scope (aim), an "E" on a convict with a bull's head, and a duck. This gives you the Memory Object consisting of aim+E+bull+con+duck.

Amiable Conduct.

It's a weird image, isn't it? But as you'll learn, the weirder the Memory Object, the easier it is to remember.

This example demonstrates that a Memory Object may consist of multiple things. In fact, it's normal to cluster a group of things together to form a Memory Object. Most words in the English language, especially ones with several syllables, will require it. There are many situations in which you can squeeze an entire sentence into a single Memory Object.

This might lead you to ask "If a Memory Object can be composed of several things, how can I distinguish one Memory Object from the next? Aren't all of them, side by side, just going to resemble a collection of junk?"

No, and for the following reasons:

First, as a rule, all the things you cluster to together to form a Memory Object must be in physical contact with one another.

Second, as will be discussed later, each Memory Object occupies a single Focal Point, which is a specific location within a larger Area. These Focal Points are, in general, an arm's length from one another. This will help you keep your Memory Objects segregated from one another.

Memory Objects can be used in one of three ways, depending on your needs.

USED ALONE

This is the simplest but least comprehensive method of using Memory Objects, and was promoted by art of memory commentators such as Quintillian, already mentioned. This is the construction of Memory Objects only, i.e., you are not building a memory palace. Instead, you memorize your lecture or part in whatever way suits you best (perhaps using the old-fashioned rote repetition method) but build Memory Objects for particularly difficult words, sentences, or portions of sentences. Here, the Memory Object's purpose is to help you only with the part you're struggling with. This can be particularly useful if a word is archaic (not used today) or if the sentence is structured in a way that seems illogical to you. The brain can be stubbornly resistant to memorizing something it doesn't like.

For example, imagine that you're trying to memorize this line from *A Midsummer Night's Dream*:

> *Ay me, for aught that I could ever read,*
>   *Could ever hear by tale or history,*
>   *The course of true love never did run smooth,*
>   *But either it was different in blood...*

Perhaps you have mastered all the words except "Ay me, for aught," because it just doesn't feel right. Your brain doesn't like the words or the order of them. Consequently, you create a Memory Object consisting of an eyeball shrink-wrapped into a package of meat (yuck! - but memorable!), surrounded by a rope with four knots in it. Eye-meat-four-knot = *Ay me, for aught.*

Note that this is not a memory palace (method of loci) approach because you are not placing the Memory Object in a Model (thus, there are no loci, i.e., locations). In other words, you aren't building a memory palace. You're just using Memory Objects here and there, as needed, and they exist in your mind independent of one another.

If this is your only need, you should can skip Chapters 10 through 23.

USED TOGETHER

As discussed earlier, the placement of multiple Memory Objects at strategic locations within your memory palace will help you to remember not only words, but the order of those words. A memory palace may house dozens, hundreds, or even thousands of memory objects. It is the placement of these objects, and their interactions with one another, that maintains order in what would otherwise be a very crowded and messy mental construct.

8

THE QUALITIES OF MEMORY OBJECTS

Memory Objects should have four primary qualities:

1. They must be sensible things, not intellectual things
2. They must be artificial things, not real things
3. They should be strange
4. They should be personal

SENSIBLE THINGS

What do I mean by *sensible?* Probably not what you think. Today, sensible means reasonable, or practical, or prudent. Saving money for retirement is a sensible thing to do, for example. If a brother is about to do something stupid, you might warn him to "be sensible," or to "come to your senses!"

But we're not going to use that modern definition of the word. We're going to use *sensible* as it was originally used, particularly by students of memory palaces. It's a usage that makes more...well, sense.

Here it is:

Sensible = anything that can be sensed.

Or, put another way, a sensible thing is anything that can be detected by the five senses, i.e., seen, heard, touched, smelled, or tasted. The examples are almost infinite, but include things like cars, houses, flowers, people, clouds, planets, and rocks.

In *Cogitationes Privatae* ("Private Thoughts"), René Descartes (1596-1650) wrote, "as the imagination uses figures to conceive of bodies, so the intellect uses sensible bodies, like the wind and light, for representing spiritual things... Sensible things can help us to conceive of Olympian things: the wind signifies the spirit, motion of time signifies life, light signifies understanding, heat signifies love, and sudden activity signifies creation."

INTELLECTUAL THINGS

Aren't all things sensible? No. Consider, for example, morality. You know what morality is, but what does it look like? Taste like? What does it sound like? Can it fall off a shelf and hit you on the head? What is its color? Its texture? What are its dimensions? How many moralities can you fit into a shoebox?

Morality is undetectable by the senses. It is an intellectual concept. Things like morality, courage, fear, envy, and justice, which cannot be sensed by the five senses, are called intellectual things. In his discussion on memory palaces, Sir Francis Bacon wrote, "Emblems bring down intellectual things to sensible things; for what is sensible, always strikes the Memory stronger, and sooner expresses itself, than what is intellectual."

In other words, it is easier to remember a sensible thing, such as a sword, than an intellectual thing, such as chivalry. In fact, I would wager that many of you, upon reading the word *chivalry*, immediately thought of a medieval knight.

Why? Because a knight is sensible. We know from books and movies what knights looked like. We envision them in suits of armor. We can hear the clang of the armor as they walk. We can imagine the sun glinting off their plate mail. We imagine them rescuing damsels or facing off against one another with lances.

Knights are emblems of chivalry. They are sensible things. Chivalry is not sensible. It has no physical appearance, or smell, or taste. It makes no sound and cannot be touched. It is an intellectual thing.

ARTIFICIAL THINGS (MEMORY OBJECTS)

Memory Objects are things that don't already exist at a location within your Model. In other words, they are not real. Memory Objects are things that you mentally add to your Model for the sole purpose of helping you memorize words. They are part of what's called artificial memory.

Let's revisit your kitchen counter, and let's assume that you are halfway through a lecture and need to remember the word "canopy," as in "canopy of heaven." To accomplish this, you might envision a can of peas on your counter. Can-of-peas = Can-o-py. This can of peas is a Memory Object because you added it to your kitchen counter in your mind to remind you of the word canopy. It is an artificial thing because the can of peas doesn't exist in the real world at the location you imagined it.

REAL THINGS (BACKGROUND OBJECTS)

The Model you select for your memory palace is based on a real place which is obviously full or real things, like furniture, paintings, photographs, shelves, televisions, and appliances. It's important that you remember those things are not Memory Objects. These are *background* objects. They are part of your Model. Your couch is just a couch. Your coffeemaker is just a coffeemaker. These real-world, pre-existing objects are in your Model by coincidence. You didn't put them there to help you remember anything.

Background objects exist in your natural memory. You remember them without effort. Your bed, for example. You've probably never stood at your bedroom doorway and concentrated on the location of your bed for fear of forgetting where it is. You don't study the location of your couch, or refrigerator, or shower. Your brain records the existence and placement of real things automatically – car keys being a mysterious exception.

Put another way, real objects are passively remembered; artificial objects are actively imagined.

Let's assume you're using your home as your Model. Think of your kitchen and zoom in on your kitchen counter. Think of everything that is currently on your counter, right now.

That might include a cookie jar, or a coffeemaker, or a dish rack. Because such things already exist on your kitchen counter in the real world, they are considered background objects. Your cookie jar is there to hold cookies, not to remind you of a word. Your coffeemaker is for making coffee. You aren't creating these objects with your imagination. You're remembering them because they are real.

Does this mean that you need to remove background objects from your Model? Not at all. Leave them just as they are. Background objects play important roles in memory palaces. Of greatest importance, they help you distinguish one Space from another.

Per *Ad Herennium*:

> "...backgrounds differing in form and nature must be secured, so that, thus distinguished, they may be clearly visible; for if a person has adopted many [similar] spaces, their resemblance to one another will so confuse him that he will no longer know what he has set in each background."

If you have three bedrooms in an empty and unfurnished house, it can be difficult to distinguish one from the other two in your mind. They're all empty, featureless cubes. But furnished rooms are easy to distinguish from one another because each will have unique furniture, wall decorations, linen, etc.

Background objects are also helpful in dividing Areas into Focal Points. It is difficult to navigate a blank, featureless wall. There are no reference points. But most walls decorated with paintings, clocks, photographs, certificates, and so forth, are easy to navigate. Each of those decorations can be used as a reference point, or basis for a Focal Point.

Background objects can also be used as props. Consider the example of a real-life cookie jar. Though the cookie jar in your kitchen can't be a Memory Object (it is a real thing, not an imagined thing), you can place your Memory Objects on the cookie jar, or under it, or inside it. You can paint an image of your Memory Object on the front of the cookie jar.

Use the background objects in your Model to your advantage. Just understand that they cannot be used as Memory Objects.

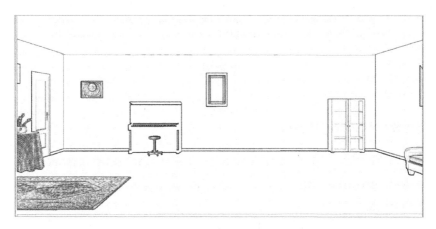

Background objects. All of the furnishings shown in the illustration above (rug, piano, shelves, window, painting, etc.) are considered background objects because they really exist and were not imagined by you. Background objects can help you navigate from one place to another but do not represent words.

Memory Objects. I've put a random Memory Object (an artificial thing) against the background of the same Area. Normally you'll have several Memory Objects for each Area. Only the conspicuous, weird-looking figure in the center is a Memory Object. In your mind, this strange thing could represent several words (perhaps three, based on the fiery globe, the sun-head, and the rod of Hermes). Every other thing in this illustration is a background object.

STRANGE THINGS

For a Memory Object to stick and for it not to be mistaken as a background object, it should be as strange and absurd as possible.

Crazy. Wacky. Ridiculous. *Insane.*

That's because the brain loves stimulation. Weird things are stimulating. Mundane things are not. Weird things are worth pondering, storing, and contemplating. Mundane things are filed away in the "been there, done that" section of your brain, and lost in the shuffle.

This is why the unknown author of the *Ad Herennium* wrote that Memory Objects should be conspicuous, "so that we can grasp and embrace them easily," and why William Preston wrote, "Everything that strikes the eye more immediately engages the attention, and imprints on the memory serious and solemn truths."

Luckily, your imagination loves nutty things. Remember that last dream you had? The one in which you were driving a cement truck through the rings of Saturn because you were late to a Christmas party and your magical teleportation ring wasn't working?

Yep, that's the kind of crazy you need to make these memory palace objects work.

PERSONAL THINGS

It's important that you conjure most of your own Memory Objects. I will provide some sample Memory Objects in the Appendix simply to illustrate how they might be composed, but the best Memory Objects are the ones you create.

In his 1582 book, *De Umbris Idearum* ("On the Shadows of Ideas"), Giordano Bruno writes, "The sensation of heat does not feel the same to everyone, but depends mostly on the degree of one's sensitivity to it. For that same reason, you should devise your images [Memory Objects] from practice...not from the insights of others which you will be unable to share."

The author of *Ad Herennium* agrees. "Why do we wish to rob anybody of his initiative, so that, to save him from making any search himself, we deliver to him everything searched out and ready? One person is more struck by one likeness, and another person by another likeness. For example, when we publicly declare that one person looks like another, many listeners will disagree, because everyone perceives things differently. The same is true with respect to images [Memory Objects]: one that seems a good choice to you or me could appear a bad choice to others. Every person, therefore, should devise his own images, suitable to his own perception."

In other words, no one can tell you what Memory Objects you should use. What works great for me, or for another brother, might not work at all for you. What works for you might not work for me. That doesn't mean you have to avoid all suggestions or examples. It only means that you should never feel obligated to use a Memory Object someone else has created.

If it works for you, great, but if it doesn't, ignore it and find something that does.

9
HOW TO CREATE MEMORY OBJECTS

Though creating Memory Objects can be fun, most of the time it's a tedious process. But here's the thing: it needs to be tedious. Memory Objects that are easily created are also easily forgotten, while those that require you to rack your brain will be more easily remembered. Do not be discouraged by the effort required. It is a good thing. It forces your brain to map things in new and different ways. It burns new trails, which is exactly what you need.

In general, I have found Memory Objects to fall into one of the following categories:

1. Like objects: homonyms, homophones, homographs, and rhymes.
2. Reminder objects: examples, samples, emblems, symbols, hieroglyphs, etc.

3. Acronyms: use of the first letter of two or more words to create a Memory Object.
4. Associated objects: objects that indirectly help you remember a word or words.

Less common, but also useful:

1. Gestures and signals objects: objects (often people) performing a gesture or sign
2. Position objects: objects that are positioned to remind you of a word such as "on" or "in" or "above."
3. Color objects: the color of an object reminds you of a word
4. Emotional or Passion-based objects: objects that elicit an emotion or passion that reminds you of a word or words
5. Repetitive or Multi-sided objects: objects are repeated or multi-sided to indicate plurals or numbers
6. Four-Sense objects: objects that use smell, taste, texture, or sound, to remind you of a word or concept, instead of, or in addition to, sight
7. People objects: objects that use a person's personal characteristics or name to remind you of a word

In the following pages, I'll explain what these are. Don't feel that you need to remember any of this, though. I'm only providing this information to help you get started, or perhaps as a reference if you get stumped somewhere down the road.

SOME GENERAL GUIDANCE:

Memory Objects don't have to match up perfectly with the words you're trying to memorize. They almost never will, in fact. I use a wok to remember the word "what." Is wok spelled with a "t" at the end? No. But that doesn't matter. It's close enough.

"One Memory Object = One Word" is NOT a rule. You can use two Memory Objects to remember one word, or you can use one Memory Object for two or more words. In fact, there are times that I struggle to come up with a suitable object for a single word, but find that I can easily create an object if I add either the following or previous word (or both). Again, there are no rules.

If you think your Memory Object is weak, double-down. If, for example, you decided to imitate my use of a wok as an object for the word "what," but your brain struggles with the association, you could think up some alternatives and combine them. "White" is close to "what," right? So, you could improve the Memory Object by making it a gleaming white wok. I don't know that I've ever seen a white wok – they're usually black or just plain steel. A white wok is definitely unusual, and something you'll remember, and the combination of white+wok might do a better job of triggering the word you're trying to remember than just the wok alone.

Don't be afraid to fuse Memory Objects together, Frankenstein style. I frequently combine an entire sentence of words into one ugly cluster of Memory Objects at one Focal Point. This is made easier if I'm using a person as one of my objects. In addition to whatever word or words that person represents, I can add objects to his or her head, hands, feet, chest, stomach, etc., and use that one Focal Point to hold a sentence or more of words.

Don't fight your mind. If your mind's eye shows you a background that differs from reality, don't try to correct it. There must be a reason your mind wants to alter your memory of what a background really looks like. You'll find that it sometimes removes features that really exist, like furniture, or alters their size or color, or blurs them until they're almost unrecognizable. Just go with it. The background is supposed to be blurry and out of focus. It's your Memory Objects that matter.

Skip articles like "the," "an," "a," etc., if you can remember them without a Memory Object. If you find through practice that you continue to get them wrong, then create them as-needed.

Finally, the internet is your best friend when trying to create Memory Objects! If you are absolutely stumped and unable to come up with Memory Object for a word, simply do an internet search on the word and look at the image results. If that doesn't work, do an internet search using a phrase such as "rhymes with (word)," or "(word) homophone," etc. If that doesn't work, go to a website that helps you create acronyms from words, or provides words containing certain letters, or…well, there are simply a lot of things you can do with the internet that ancient users of the memory palace could only dream about.

That said, I strongly recommend that you first try to develop your Memory Objects without the internet. Objects that occur to you without help are the best, more memorable objects. Also, the effort of struggling to find a Memory

Object is itself a positive exercise that will seat the corresponding word in your brain.

HOMONYM OBJECTS

A homonym is a word that has the same spelling as another word, but a different meaning. For example, "wind." You can wind a piece of string around your finger. Wind turns a windmill. A trail can wind into the woods. Thus, if you wanted to remember the word wind, you could use as your Memory Object the key used to wind up a mechanical clock or the handle used to wind up a toy.

HOMOPHONE OBJECTS

A homophone is a word that sounds like another word but is spelled differently and has a different meaning. For example, you eat two hamburgers. You can go to France. You can go to their party. You promise to be there. Thus, you could use the numeral "2" as a Memory Object for the word "to."

HOMOGRAPH OBJECTS

Homographs are two words that are spelled the same, but mean different things and are pronounced differently. For example, you can eat ice cream and be content. You can read the label of a can to determine its contents. Old houses have lead pipes. Commanders lead troops into battle. If you were looking for a Memory Object for the verb "tie," (as in, "we are tied to our fraternity") you could use a man's tie.

RHYMING OBJECTS

Words that rhyme sound similar, but not necessarily identical, when spoken. The pronunciation or spelling of your Memory Object does not have to exactly correlate with that of the words to be remembered. Sometimes it's sufficient that a Memory Object merely rhymes with what you're trying to remember. For example, "see that" can be remembered as a CPAP mask, or a seabass. The Memory Object for "purpose" can be a porpoise.

REMINDER OBJECTS

A reminder object is a powerful reminder of the word to be memorized. For example, a clock is a very good reminder of the word "time." Wings can be used to remember the word "fly." Thus, a clock with wings attached could serve as an object to remind you that "time flies."

The principles of Freemasonry are often taught indirectly, through the use of reminder objects like emblems, symbols, and hieroglyphs. While this is often perceived as a way of guarding secret teachings, often such devices are used because our principles are too complex to capture in words. Sometimes a picture is worth a thousand words, while at other times it expresses something that cannot be described by words.

It is difficult for most people to distinguish between an "emblem" and "symbol," but there is a difference, which you, as a Freemason, should understand.

As Br. Albert G. Mackey noted, "Emblem is very generally used as synonymous with symbol, although the two words do not express exactly the same meaning. An emblem is properly a representation of an idea by a visible object...but a symbol is more extensive in its application, includes every representation of an idea by an image, whether that image is presented immediately to the senses as a visible and tangible substance, or only brought before the mind by words."

Within the lectures, an emblem is usually an object that is used to represent a concept or principle. For example, the beehive is an emblem of industry. Worker bees swarming around a hive are industrious, so there's a logical correlation between the image and the concept. Similarly, death is emblematically represented by a coffin, for obvious reasons.

More broadly, however, a symbol doesn't have to be logically related to the thing it represents. For example, the exclamation point (!) is generally recognized as a symbol of emphasis or alarm, despite the fact that it's merely a dot with a vertical line over it. If you were a visitor from another planet and was shown an exclamation point by itself, with no context, you'd never guess its meaning.

The same could be said of the famous "peace" symbol, a circle bisected by a vertical line, with two additional lines extending from its center to its edges, terminating at the 4 o'clock and 8 o'clock positions. Asked to identify this image, most anyone alive after 1960 would immediately say "Peace!" It's an image often painted on signs (or the faces) of peace activists.

Yet almost anyone who died before 1960 would probably have been stumped. Given a hundred guesses, it's unlikely they'd have ever associate the image with *peace*. There would just be no reason for them to have done so. The peace symbol was designed in 1958 as a symbol for nuclear disarmament. Its designer based the image on the position of flags used by sailors to communicate the letters "N" and "D" to distant ships. One flag pointed at the sky and another at the ground, forming a vertical line, communicated "N." A flag held to either side a pointed at the ground at an angle, forming an inverted "V," communicated the letter "D." Thus, the position of signaling flags used by sailors was transformed into the image of circle containing a vertical line and inverted V, which became the symbol of nuclear disarmament. Only later did the symbol's meaning expand from "no nuclear weapons" to "no war of any kind."

The only reason we today associate this image - a symbol - with "peace" is that we have been taught to. It's a convention, or something we've simply agreed to, as a society. Unlike an emblem, it doesn't have to make sense.

ACRONYM OBJECTS

An acronym is an abbreviation created from the initial letters of words. For example, "U.S.A." is the acronym for "United States of America." Acronyms can make great Memory Objects because they allow you to squeeze a lot of words into a single Memory Object. What makes them less-than-great is that you have to remember what the words are, with only the first letter as a hint.

For the purposes of a memory palace, the acronym needs to help spell a word that can be represented by a Memory Object.

A few examples:

Wisdom, Strength, and Beauty = WaSaBi (a wasabi pea)

Square, Level, and Plumb = SLiP (a slip of paper, a pay slip, or a woman's slip)

LETTER-LIKE OBJECTS

This is an alternative to Acronym Objects. Instead of turning an acronym into an object, you can find a single object that resembles a letter. For example, the letter "A" resembles a tent or truss; "C" looks like an open cuff bracelet; "F" a monkey wrench; "G" a clamp; "I" a column; etc. Thus, you could remember "Fellowcraft" as a monkey wrench clinching a bracelet.

For a Renaissance example of this technique, do an internet search for images related to Johannes Romberch's *Congestorium Artificiose Memorie* (effectively, "Encyclopedia of Artificial Memory"). If you're looking for something more practical, simply do an internet search for, "Things that look like letters."

ASSOCIATED OBJECTS

This one is abstract and hard to categorize, but it's the use of any object to remind you of a word through association. For example, I almost always use a snake to remember the word "is." Why? "Snake" doesn't sound like "is." A snake isn't a symbol or emblem for the word "is." And S.N.A.K.E. obviously isn't an acronym for the word "is."

No, I use a snake because a snake *hisses*. "Hiss" reminds me of "is." I associate a snake with the sound it makes, and the sound the word we use for the sound it makes, "hiss," sounds like the word I want to remember.

GESTURES AND SIGNALS OBJECTS

If you're a Freemason, I probably don't need to provide any examples of what these objects might consist of. Suffice to say these objects would probably be in the form of a person making a sign or gesture which you would recognize. But gestures and signals are not reserved for Freemasons. Gestures any person might recognize include a wave of the hand in greeting (perhaps used to remember the word "by" in lieu of "bye"), two fingers on a hand upright in a peace symbol ("peace"), hands over eyes ("blind" or "darkness"), a finger held vertically over the lips ("silence"), etc.

POSITION OBJECTS

The position of an object can also be used. For example, the Memory Object of a vase with a B painted on it (used to remember the word "base"), set atop a book, can be used to memorize the phrase, "based on a book."

Notice that in that example I've used both a "sounds like" object ("vase" sounds like "base") and a "reminder object" (a book is...well, a book).

COLOR OBJECTS

These have a more limited application but are worth keeping in mind. In their simplest form, the color of objects can help you remember words. A very simple example would be the use of a red "C" as a Memory Object for "Red Sea." You could also develop a system in which colors had numeric values. If you have two or more Spaces that look alike in real life, you could mentally paint the walls of each Space a different color to distinguish them. Robert Fludd, for example, divided his Model (he used a theater) into black and white Spaces and painted each of the columns in the Spaces a different color.

EMOTION OR PASSION BASED OBJECTS

Several memory palace proponents, today and in centuries past, recommend that you choose Memory Objects which trigger an emotional or passionate response, such as love, anger, lust, repulsion, sadness, or excitement. Bruno states that objects which "stir up the emotions" can "open the doors of memory," while the author of *Ad Herennium* suggests that we use disfigured, bloodied, or comic figures.

In 1600, Peter of Ravenna, apparently not averse to controversy, frankly stated, "I usually fill my memory-places with the images of beautiful women…I hope chaste and religious men will pardon me." Yates thought it possible that Dante's Inferno, with its myriad levels and torments, "could be regarded as a kind of memory system for memorizing Hell and its punishments, with striking images on orders of places…"

REPETITIVE OR MULTI-SIDED OBJECTS

It is sometimes helpful to repeat Memory Objects to remind you words are plural. For example, if you were trying to memorize "the three tenants" and decided to use a tent as your Memory Object, you would picture three tents, side-by-side. Similarly, using triangles, squares, hexagons, etc., to remember numbers is an ancient practice. A triangle = 3, square = 4, hexagon = 5, etc. A triangle is often used in art in connection to the Christian Trinity. A circle may be used as a marker for "infinity."

OBJECTS TIED TO THE OTHER FOUR SENSES

Not surprisingly, when we use our "mind's eye," we imagine how a Memory Object appears. Put another way, we use phantom sight. The object doesn't exist, but we "see" it in our mind. Memory palaces are highly reliant on sight, both real and imagined. But that doesn't mean we should ignore the other four senses, namely, hearing, smell, touch, and taste (there are arguably several other senses, but we'll stick to the five everyone knows).

Because Memory Objects are usually perceived at a distance, hearing and smell work better than touch or taste.

Excluding sight, hearing is arguably the most useful sense in a memory palace, which means sounds are most useful in constructing Memory Objects. Of course, what we are really referring to are *imagined* sounds, since the memory palace exists only in your mind. The sounds could include words spoken by people, or music, or horns, or bells. The possibilities are limited only by your imagination.

Recent studies have shown that the more senses you use to remember something, the longer it will remain in your memory. This is because each sense uses a separate brain storage region, which means if one region fails the others can rush to the rescue.

I will admit, though, that I have found very few ways to implement sound in a memory palace. Based on the scarcity of any references to sound in other texts on the art of memory, I have to assume that other users found the task equally challenging. Instinctively, I'd opine that music has the most potential. It is widely known that words are easier to memorize if put to music. The difficulty is how this can be applied to a memory palace.

The implementation of smell in creation of a Memory Object is not any easier. However, assigning a certain smell or fragrance to a Space or Area might help trigger the memory of that location's purpose. For example, you might assign the pleasant smell of roses to a Space which stores a paragraph about beauty or love, or the smell of mildew in a location related to death.

Touch is even trickier, though if allowed some latitude, I'd suggest that we allow touch to include temperature, in which case you could make a Space frigid to remind you that a paragraph includes the word "cold," or hot to remind you of the word "sun," and so forth.

PEOPLE OBJECTS

This is simply the use of people to remember words. If, for example, you are trying to remember "Worshipful Master," a logical Memory Object would be the current resident of the East. If you are memorizing the word "beauty," you could use a beautiful person. For "strength" you might imagine a weightlifter.

A less intuitive method of using people, but one suggested by several ancient authorities, is to use people's names to create acronyms. Ideally, you'd want to find a different person for each letter of the alphabet, the letter being the initial of his or her first or last name. A person named Alfred could be

A, while Bill would be B, etc. Assuming you had a person for every letter, you could place these people next to one another to remind you of a word.

Thus, if the word you wanted to memorize was "fate," you could imagine Fred, Alfred, Tom, and Eddie standing together, or (to save room), a photograph of them standing in that order.

SOLOMON'S MEMORY PALACE

An illustration from "A Collection of Emblems," by George Wither, 1625 printing. A modern translation of the old English used in the author's explanation of the emblem would be, "A troubled mind is one that desires something but is paralyzed between great hopes and great fears. This is expressed as a Smoking Heart placed between a Fastened Anchor and a Bended Bow to which a Barbed-Arrow is fixed. The bow's string pulled taut and ready to release the arrow. The Smoke signals burning desire. The Anchor represents Hope, which keep despair at bay. The bow and arrow signify Fear, which perpetually frightens the Soul. They who can control their desires (whether good or bad) in seeking Pleasures, are at peace, because they are not disturbed by Fear."

10

THE MODEL

- Model > Spaces > Areas > Focal Points
- Section > Paragraphs > Sentences > Words

The first thing you need to construct a memory palace is a Model. This is a mental image of a location, typically a building and/or the land around that building, that you are extremely familiar with. It needs to be a place that you can describe in great detail with almost no effort.

Your home is an ideal Model. If you and I were sitting in a restaurant, and I asked you to give me a step-by-step description of your home, starting at the front door, you could. You would be able to describe, in incredible detail, what I'd see as soon as I stepped inside. You could describe the color of the walls, what was hanging on the walls, the location of the electrical outlets, light switches, flooring type, and what I'd see if I looked around. You could probably describe every major scuff or stain on the floor or dent in the drywall.

You could tell me approximately how about many steps I'd need to take in a certain direction to get to the first room, and then you could probably spend an hour describing every detail of that room (its dimensions, color, smell, temperature, contents, etc.).

If I waited a month and asked you to give me a verbal tour all over again, the description would be almost the same, assuming you hadn't done any redecorating. You'd rephrase some things, sure, but on a whole, what you told me would be consistent with what you told me the month before.

Think about that. When it comes to your home, you're a genius. Without even trying, you've stored tens of thousands of details in your brain that you can summon at will. A memory palace taps into that genius by piggy-backing on your natural ability to remember how to get from one place to another and details about the places you've been.

STRUCTURE

Your Model is a lot like directories on a computer. Items stored on a computer's hard drive are organized in a prescribed manner. At the top level there are directories, and within those directors are folders, and within those folders are subfolders, and within those folders might be still more subfolders, and within those sub-folders are files.

Your memory palace is set up in a similar manner:

Models (locations) = Directories

Spaces (yards, gardens, rooms, etc.) = Folders

Areas (floor, wall, corner, etc.) = Subfolders

Focal Points (a specific spot on the wall, floor, etc.) = Lower level subfolders

WITH THIS ANALOGY IN MIND, HERE'S ONE WAY IN WHICH A palace can be constructed:

Models = Sections to be memorized (part, role, lecture, etc.)

Spaces = Paragraphs
Areas = Sentences
Focal Points = Words

CAPACITY

You might wonder whether a Model has sufficient capacity to hold all the information you need to memorize.

Let's assume you're using a house as the Model for your memory palace. To keep things simple, we'll use only indoor Spaces. A typical American home consists of three bedrooms, two bathrooms, a basement, kitchen, and a family room.

That's eight rooms. Each room is a Space, and each Space holds about one "paragraph."

Each room has four walls, a ceiling, and a floor. These are called Areas, and each Area holds about eight Focal Points, which are simply any portion of an Area that you can "zoom in" on. For example, a nail where you'd hang a photograph. Each Focal Point will be the home of a Memory Object, which represents one to four words.

Do the math. 8 Spaces x 6 Areas per Space x 8 Focal Points per Area x 3 words per Focal Point = 1,152 words.

Thus, a small memory palace created by a beginner can

hold, at a minimum, more than a thousand words. The U.S. Declaration of Independence contains approximately 1,300 words. The average number of words on a book page is about 250. A little math will show that even the simplest memory palace could thus "hold" six pages of the average book.

If we were serious, though, we'd include other Spaces, to include outdoor Spaces, and indoor Spaces such as hallways, garages, and closets. This would allow us to easily triple the number of words memorized to around 5,000. That is more than sufficient to hold any section of work that you'll need to memorize as a Freemason.

That may not be enough for all of your needs, but the sky is the limit if you have enough Models. In fact, one famous memory palace builder, Francesco Panigarola (1548-1594), an Italian Franciscan, is said to have developed palaces that contained, in total, almost 100,000 Spaces!

Suitable Models

Your home can be a great Model because it is deeply impressed upon your memory. Assuming you've lived in your home for a while, you can mentally "walk" from one room to another and envision every piece of furniture along the way. That's important, because you need to reserve your brainpower for the creation of Memory Objects.

Your Model doesn't have to be your home, though. You can use any home (your parents' home, for example, or a friend's). It can be a home you live in now, or a home you lived in before. It can be either a house or an apartment, though the average apartment might be a bit tight for your needs.

For larger, more complicated memory palaces, I'd suggest

you use as your Model your favorite supermarket, school, college, department store, or shopping mall. Some users of this technique use neighborhoods, or parks, or city shopping districts as Models. I personally find such large locations problematic, but every brain works a bit differently. Use whatever works best for you. The most important thing in choosing a Model is that you must be able to use your mind's eye to move easily from one location to another without getting lost.

Below are some additional suggestions on how to select your Model, based on my experiences and those historical texts which are generally considered authoritative.

1. For your first Mind Palace, I'd suggest using the interior of a building, not an outdoor location. Buildings are ideal Models for memory palaces because navigating them is easy. The rooms are divided by walls, and your movement from one room to another is constrained by stairs, corridors, and doors. If I were to ask you how to get from one room to another inside a home you're familiar with, you could tell me with confidence what other rooms I'd go through or pass along the way. There might be two or three ways to travel from one point to another but the possibilities are finite.

Additionally, rooms in buildings are usually cubes that offer six distinct Areas (four walls, the ceiling, and the floor). An Area, like a wall, is used to store one or more sentences but should be able to hold at least one. Few paragraphs contain more than six sentences, so a cube is the perfect shape for a Space.

Finally, interior Models come with a lot of background stuff, like furniture, wall hangings, windows, etc. These background items can help you remember the order of your Memory Objects.

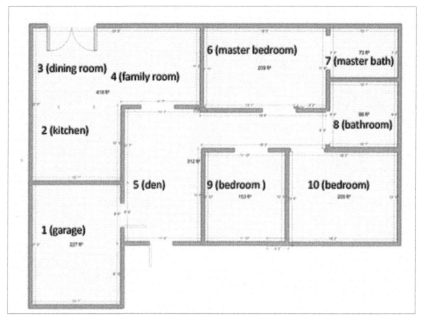

A Model. This example home (being used as a Model) has ten rooms (which are Spaces). In general, a Model should have a number of Spaces equal to the number of paragraphs you are memorizing.

OUTDOOR MODELS

Outdoor Models (in the past, sometimes referred to as "Fields") can be more difficult.

First, there is the problem of navigation. Buildings are like mazes with only a limited number of turns available to you, but outdoor Models are usually devoid of obstacles, which means you have an almost infinite number of ways to get from one point to another. To navigate an outdoor Model, you need to set waypoints to ensure you always travel along the same path, and you need to remember what those waypoints are.

Second, deciding what to use as a Space is more challenging outdoors. A garden is a good Space, as is a driveway, porch, and patio. Though these features don't have walls, they are sufficiently large and usually four edges, giving them the shape of a room.

But if you opt to use a tree, mailbox, or birdhouse as a Space, you'll have to imagine that the Space includes both the feature at the center and the ground around it. This usually requires that you imagine a perimeter barrier of some kind. That perimeter is invisible in the real world, unlike the walls of a room, and so is less memorable.

Again, this is not an insurmountable obstacle – I have several outdoor Models – but it takes a little extra work. Keep things simple in your first attempt, and restrict yourself to an indoor location if possible.

Outdoor Spaces might be as large as a front or back yard, or as small as a porch, patio, gate, garden, bush, sidewalk, driveway, swimming pool, or fire pit. However, every Space needs about 100 sq. ft. to do its job, so if you were to select a gate as a Space, you'd really be selecting the gate and the ground in front, behind, and to either side of it. When choosing an outdoor Space, be sure that it's got enough empty ground around it to serve its purpose.

SOLOMON'S MEMORY PALACE

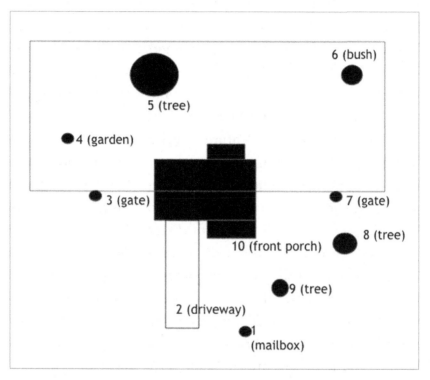

Outdoor Model. Any outdoor location can be used as a Model (you may also combine indoor and outdoor locations into a single Model. For outdoor models, you select features that can serve as Spaces. In this example, the yard around a house has ten Spaces, which should be sufficient to hold ten paragraphs.

2. Your Model should not be "busy." Airport terminals, railway stations, and football stadiums are "busy." As a rule of thumb, if you can't think of a location without also thinking of people swarming around it, it's not a good location to use in a memory palace, because all that movement is distracting. As Bruno wrote, "It is important to have a clear view with excellent light, for dense darkness, great crowds, scenes that fade into the distance, and such things prevent clear preservation of the scene."

This point was made centuries earlier, in *Ad Herennium*: "It will be more advantageous to obtain backgrounds in a deserted than in a populous region, because the crowding and passing to and fro of people confuse and weaken the impress of the images, while solitude keeps their outlines sharp."

3. Each Space (discussed in detail in the next chapter) within your Model should be unique. In most cases, this won't be a problem. If you're using a house, the furniture will be different in each room. In a supermarket, each aisle will carry a different product (coffee, meat, etc.). This is important, because if the Spaces are too alike, they might blur in your memory, and you might confuse one with another. Examples of bad Spaces would include an unfurnished cubicle farm in an office building, a snow-covered plain, and a corn field.

4. The Model should be neither too large nor too small for your needs. A small shed is a poor choice, as is the Pacific Ocean. The first doesn't give you enough real estate and the second gives you too much.

5. It should be brightly illuminated. This might sound odd, since you're only imagining yourself walking through the Model. But a location that is dimly lit in real life will be dimly lit in your mind, also. Objects in dimly lit Spaces - in the real

world, or in your mind - are hard to see. True, you could try to imagine a bright light shining on an Area that is dark, but in doing so you'd be wasting precious brain power. Just avoid these locations and focus on locations that are well illuminated.

6. It should be dedicated to a single section of material. In other words, try to avoid using a single Model for multiple palaces. Some people can do this, but from my experience, each Model should be dedicated to a single purpose. For example, my house is my Model for the third section lecture of the Entered Apprentice degree, while a supermarket is my Model for the third section lecture of the Master Mason's degree. Using my house as the Model for both lectures would have been confusing. And yes, that means that whenever I buy groceries I sometimes end up reciting a portion of the lecture to myself.

7. It should be based on a real location, but can be based on a fictional location. Should you ever exhaust your supply of real-world Models for your memory palaces, you can create one from your imagination. For example, you could use building or urban Area from a video game you're very familiar with, or a movie, or a book, or you could create a completely new place, perhaps using paper and pencil or a computer-aided design program.

In fact, *Ad Herennium* provides for just this situation when it states, "Although it is easy for a person with a relatively large experience to equip himself with as many and as suitable backgrounds as he may desire, even a person who believes that he finds no store of backgrounds that are good enough, may succeed in fashioning as many such as he wishes. For the imagination can embrace any region whatsoever and in it at will fashion and construct the setting of some background. Hence, if we are not content with our ready-made supply of backgrounds, we may in our imagination create a region for ourselves and obtain a most serviceable distribution of appropriate backgrounds."

That said, I'd strongly recommend against using a purely fictional Model until you really have exhausted all real locations because creating a Model from scratch requires a lot of extra work. More importantly, my experience has been that imagined Models are less reliable than Models based on real places. It appears other practitioners have had similar issues with fictional Models. In *Tomas secundus...de supernaturali*, Robert Fludd warns against creating fictional Models because "confusion will result, the uncertainties and wanderings of your mind overwhelming your ability to concentrate."

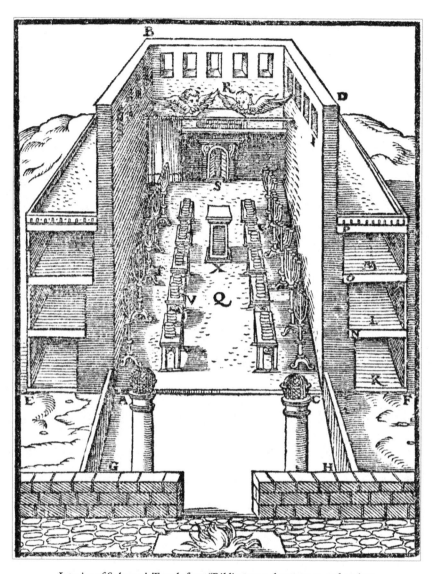

Interior of Solomon's Temple from "Bibliorvm codex sacer et avthenticvs, Testamenti vtriusq[ue] Veteris & Noui ex Hebræa & Græca veritate, quàm proximè ad literam quidem fieri potuit, fidelissimè translatus in linguam Latinam: de vniuersa huius operis ratione, differetur in subiecta praefatione," by Sante Pagnini (1470-1541).

II
SPACES

- Model > Spaces > Areas > Focal Points
- Section > Paragraphs > Sentences > Words

God called to Adam and asked, "Where are you?"
- Genesis 3: 9

Spaces are correlated to paragraphs. Spaces have three dimensions, which can be measured in terms of length, width, and height. The ideal shape of a Space is a cube.

In the English language, we divide written documents into paragraphs, with each paragraph usually dedicated to a specific topic or sub-topic, though sometimes we need to break unusually long paragraphs into smaller ones for the sake of readability. In a memory palace, each topic or sub-topic is assigned to a Space, which is usually a room (indoors), or a feature (outdoors).

There is an exception to this guidance, however. There are some Masonic works that are not in paragraph form. In appearance, these look more like scripts. If you're trying to memorize one of those works, you can treat the entire page as if it was just one paragraph, i.e. a Space can be used to store a page of information.

INDOOR SPACES

Indoor Spaces are usually rooms, but you could expand this category to include hallways, foyers, closets, or any other distinctive locations. Indoor spaces are not necessarily rooms, however. For example, a Model grocery store will be divided into aisles, not rooms, in which case each aisle or department might be considered an Area. If your model is a gym, the Spaces could be based on the type of equipment that is at a certain location, i.e., the free weights Space, the treadmill Space, the basketball Space, etc. An office may have cubicles for Spaces.

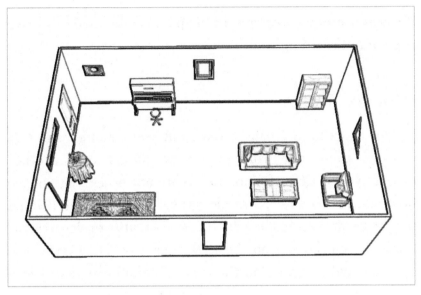

Indoor Space. A single average-sized room is a Space. In general, one Space is needed for each paragraph to be memorized.

SOLOMON'S MEMORY PALACE

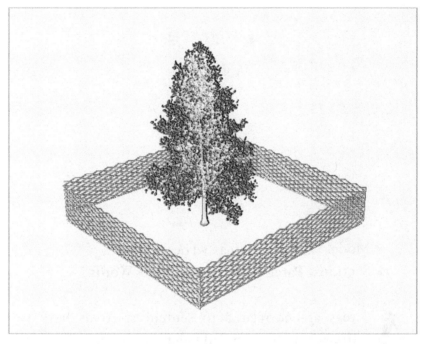

Outdoor Space. Identifying outdoor Spaces is more difficult than for indoor Spaces because you must often imagine some kind of perimeter. The easiest way to do this may be to imagine a fence rising up from a square perimeter using the four points of the compass as a guide.

12
AREAS

- Model > Spaces > Areas > Focal Points
- Section > Paragraphs > Sentences > Words

Areas are correlated to sentences. Areas have two dimensions (width and height, if vertical, like a wall, or width and length if horizontal, like a floor or ceiling). The ideal shape of an Area is a square or oblong.

An Area is simply a portion of a Space. Indoors, where a Space is usually a room, an Area is normally a wall, the floor, and/or the ceiling. Thus, a square room will typically have between four and six Areas. When you first build a memory palace and use an indoor Space, you might want to stick to the four walls of a room and avoid using the floor and ceiling as Areas. It's easy to mentally scan a room from left to right; adding up and down to the mix can make you mentally dizzy.

If you have an Area that is unusually large, such as a grocery store aisle, break it up into smaller components. For example, if "Aisle 3" includes rice, pasta, and bean sections, let each of those sections be an Area, for a total of three Areas.

As stated earlier, Areas are more difficult to define in outdoor Spaces. Each edge of a porch or driveway can be an Area, or each row in a vegetable garden. Less intuitively, you could imagine a large circle or square around a tree or mailbox, and designate each cardinal point (north, south, east, west) as an Area.

When you assign a perimeter to an outside Space, you are also implicitly imagining a plane, i.e., a two-dimensional surface rising from, and perpendicular to, the perimeter line. Put another way, you are imagining that there is an invisible wall rising up from the square or circle you've designated as your perimeter, turning a square into a cube, or a circle into a cylinder.

If this sounds confusing, drop it. It's not that important.

Use whatever you are comfortable with and be creative.

BOB W. LINGERFELT

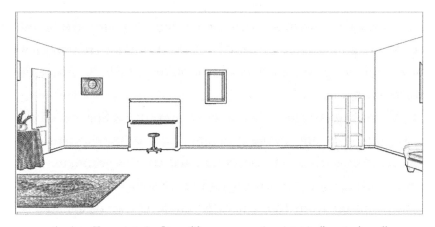

An Area. For an interior Space, like a room, an Area is typically a single wall. The wall with the piano against it would be one Area. The walls to either side would also be Areas, and the wall opposite it (for a total of four Areas). Note that the floor and ceiling may also be areas (increasing the total to six Areas). In general, an Area should be able to hold at least one sentence.

13
FOCAL POINTS

- Model > Spaces > Areas > Focal Points
- Section > Paragraphs > Sentences > Words

Focal Points are correlated to a word or words. Focal Points have a single dimension, the point at which a Memory Object for the word or words resides.

Whether you're indoors or outdoors, you rarely look at a complete Area. For example, if you're in your living room, you almost never look at an entire wall. It's almost impossible for your eyes to take in an entire wall. Seeing an entire wall requires you to be a long distance from it (unless it's unusually small), and most Spaces just aren't deep enough to give you that distance. Instead of seeing the wall, you instead focus on a specific point, allowing the Area around that point to blur. Camera lenses work in a similar manner.

Within a memory palace, we call this a Focal Point. A Focal Point in a memory palace is a placeholder for a word or words. When you're setting up your Model, you don't need to know what words the Focal Points will be used for. You can think of a Focal Point as a small shelf, or cubbyhole, or a nail on the wall. It's a place for the future placement of something (a Memory Object), but you don't need to decide what that something will be just yet.

An Area should be large enough to hold at least four Focal Points and probably no more than twelve. An ancient rule is that your Focal Points should not be any closer than an arm's length from one another because an Area that is too cluttered will confuse you. On the other hand, Focal Points within an Area should be no further than two arms' lengths apart, because if you put too much distance between your Focal Points, you might lose the "connection" between them. An exception to this rule if the deliberate combination of several objects to form a single Memory Object.

The average bedroom wall can hold four to five Focal Points, if they are all at the same height. Once you get more comfortable with memory palaces, you'll find that you can "stack" Focal Points. For example, an Area could have an upper level (just below the ceiling), a mid-level, and a lower level (just above the floor). Using that technique, every wall could easily host eight to ten Focal Points. I usually stack two Focal Points in a column, giving me, on average, eight Focal Points per Area.

Remember, however, that in a room, the horizontal planes (floor and ceilings) form right angles with vertical planes (walls), and each wall forms right angles with adjacent walls. The Memory objects that these Focal Points will hold are three-dimensional (they have depth), so care needs to be taken to ensure there is enough space between the wall and any grid you place on the floor or ceiling.

I would advise allowing the distance of two normal steps between all walls and any grid placed on the floor or ceiling.

YOU HAVE TWO OPTIONS WHEN ESTABLISHING YOUR FOCAL Points.

The first is to pre-designate your Focal Points as soon as you select an Area for use. This means that you will decide in advance where your Memory Objects will go, without knowing just yet what the objects will be. This might be the easiest approach if you have a crowded background.

The second option, and the one I use, is to hold off on establishing Focal Points until you know what Memory Objects you intend to use. This is a more common-sense approach since you don't know how large or complicated a Memory Object will be until you've actually created it. If you choose your Focal Points in advance, you might find that your Memory Objects crowd the Area (if they are large) or waste a lot of an Area (if they are small).

As an analogy, imagine you are remodeling your kitchen and plan to purchase new appliances and install a new sink. You can do things one of two ways. You can install all of the cabinetry, electrical outlets, lighting, and plumbing, and then hope to find appliances and a sink that will fit in the places you reserved for them, or you can select your appliances and sink and begin your remodel to accommodate them.

Use the method that works best for you.

Focal Points. In general, a Focal Point is any portion of an Area (in this case, a wall) which you can focus on. The five circles in the illustration above are only one possible configuration. However, the example does illustrate the principle that, when possible, each Focal Point should be at least an arm's length from any other Focal Point (unless the Focal Points are interacting), but no further than two arm's lengths. Also, note that I've utilized background objects (the painting for #1, the piano for #2, the window for #3, etc.) as reference or anchor points to help me remember the locations of my Focal Points.

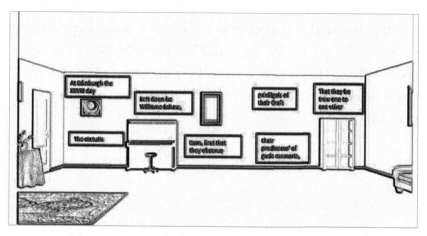

Words in Areas. This is an illustration of how words from a sentence or sentences might be divided up among the Memory Objects that you place at the Focal Points. You don't actually write the words into a picture like this. You simply select a Focal Point (for example, above and below the picture on the far left) on your Area (the wall) and then create Memory Objects to place there that will help you memorize a corresponding part of the sentence.

Consider the line, "That they be true to one another" from the First Schaw Statute of 1598. To remember those words, I could create a Memory Object consisting of a hat filled with hay, with a trowel stuck in it. A bee buzzes around the handle of the trowel and lands on a price tag dangling from it. The tag reads, "$21" and has the odd logo of an otter on it. Thus, "hat-hay-bee-trowel-2-1-an-otter." I could place that Memory Object on the background object of a bookshelf.

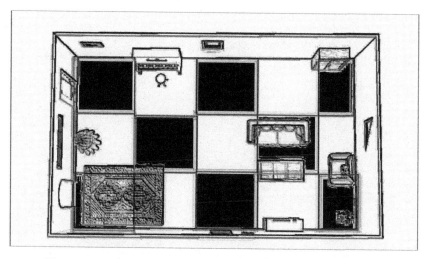

Floor Focal Points. A floor Area may be divided into Focal Points by dividing it into a grid. It may be helpful to visualize this grid as a black and white checkered surface. A 3x5 grid is used in this example, but any size may be used. The same technique can be used to divide a ceiling into Focal Points. In the example above, you might use the rug, couch, and coffee table as reference points for your Focal Points. Note that the grid does not extend to the walls of the room. This is to avoid overlapping Memory Objects on the floor with those assigned to the walls (which, though seen from the side, often sit or stand on the floor).

BOB W. LINGERFELT

SOLOMON'S MEMORY PALACE

Robert Fludd's memory palace. Note that Fludd has made use of both the vertical and horizontal Areas in this Space., but he mysteriously omitted any instructions on how, exactly, this Space should be used. It is possible that each rectangle on the walls would serve as a Focal Point, as would each square in the grid on the floor. The shapes (diamonds, circles, and six-sided polygon) are supposed to be different colors and were probably used as reference points. Each door may lead to a Space (or two Spaces, including the upper level). That there are three galleries on the left and four galleries on the right suggests the traveler was intended to move through the Model from left to right. The number of tiers, doors, and windows suggest that this would be used for list memorization of metaphysical concepts and not for verbatim memorization, though it would be equally useful for the latter. It is tied in some way to the signs of the zodiac.

14

THE HUMAN BODY

The human body can be a Memory object, or it can be used as a source for Focal Points for other Memory Objects, or it can be used for both. The human body is a map with well-established locations: hands, feet, knees, elbows, forearms, calves, stomach, chest, neck, head, ears, eyes, nose...and so on.

You can place Memory Objects at any of these locations and move from one to another in a pattern of your choosing. In the example below, I'm starting at the left foot and spiraling in to finish at the abdomen. This allows me to place fourteen Memory Objects on this person. Or, I could place as few as two – one Memory Object in each hand, perhaps.

The person can also be a Memory Object – for example, if you have a brother, he'd be a great Memory Object for the word *brother*, right?

Obviously, it's not necessary for the person to stand in the position shown in the illustration. In fact, you'd make better use of the Memory Object if the person was interacting with the Memory Objects to the left or right, since interaction cements Memory Objects together.

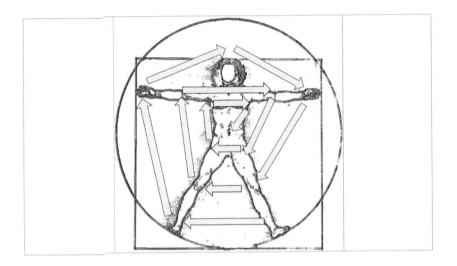

SOLOMON'S MEMORY PALACE

BELOW IS A SKETCH WHICH I USED TO MEMORIZE A NON-esoteric portion of a lecture for the EA degree in Nebraska. It teaches the importance of industry, i.e., steadily working toward worthy objectives. Put more simply: "don't be lazy." This is emblematically represented by the beehive, where the bees are almost always in motion.

I do not pretend to be an artist, and this sketch was hurriedly done, but it sufficed for my needs. Drawing it helped to burn the image into my brain.

BOB W. LINGERFELT

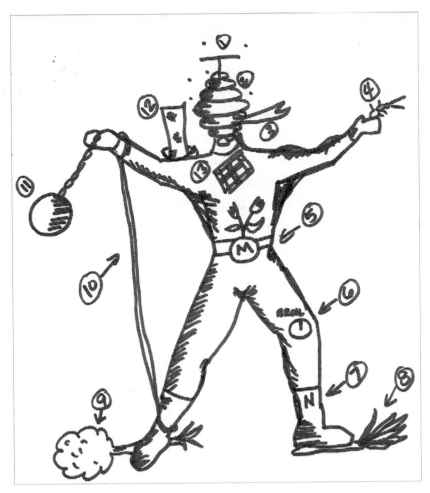

The Dreaded Beehive Monster of Nebraska

The words I wanted to memorize were: *The beehive is an emblem of industry and recommends that practice...*

I opted to use the human body to compile a few Memory Object components. They are:

1. A capital "T" at the top. It looks like an old antenna.
2. A beehive, as traditionally represented, in lieu of the head, with bees buzzing around it.
3. A long snake's tongue "hissing" from the beehive's "mouth."
4. An ant, struggling to escape the left hand.
5. A belt buckle with an "M" on it, from which flowers bloom
6. An oven dial, which I imagined could rotate the knee into different positions.
7. An "N" logo on the boot.
8. A feather duster, crushed beneath the left foot.
9. A tree, crushed beneath the right foot.
10. An elastic bend, of the type used in exercise.
11. A wrecking ball being swung on a chain by the right hand.
12. A mended top hat balanced precariously on the right bicep.
13. A piece of lattice glued to the chest.

YES, IT'S A RIDICULOUS CREATURE THAT I'VE CREATED, which is just as it should be. I imagined it as the dreaded Beehive Monster of Nebraska, hissing and crushing trees and feather dusters across the state as it swings a wrecking ball against helpless giant ants, the mended top hat on its shoulder a tragic reminder of an earlier time when the creature had a human head. The lattice stuck to the creature's chest, like the flowers blooming from its belt buckle, are from a garden that the monster recently destroyed in its terrible rampage. The monster receives its orders from its alien bee masters via the T-shaped antenna impaled in its beehive head.

Their orders? *Kill all ants!*

Preposterous! And *memorable*.

Read in a more-or-less clockwise fashion, from top to bottom, I have:

T - beehive - hiss - ant - M - bloom - oven - dust - tree - band - wreck- mends - hat - lattice

...which is, *"The beehive is an emblem of industry and recommends that practice..."*

You'll notice that I really didn't need #7, that "N" logo on the boot. #6 (oven) already had an *n* at the end. I added that to reinforce #6, in case I forgot what it represented. It's not a bad idea to layer Memory Objects or components so that they reinforce one another. When to do that is completely your call.

I also opted *not* to use several available body parts, like elbows, simply because their use didn't feel necessary or "right." My brain didn't intuitively want to place objects in those locations, so I didn't. I recommend that you do the same. Your brain is artistic. Go with the flow and don't try to insist on an image that your brain resists.

❧ 15 ❧
THE EYE

In a mind palace, we use terms such as move, navigate, and travel because they allow us to process Memory Objects in a specific order based on their spatial relationships. It is sometimes difficult to comprehend what these terms mean in an imaginary environment, however.

In the real world, after entering a room you'd have to walk around it to see all the Focal Points, or, alternatively, go to the middle of the room and pivot in a full circle while scanning the walls, floor, and ceiling.

In your memory palace, you don't have a body. Your mind's eye is more like a magical floating camera. It can see all things within your palace at all times without moving at all. It can teleport from one Space to another – or from one Model to another – instantly. It is somewhat analogous to what a computer or video gamer sees on a screen when viewing a game's environment through the eyes of the hero, assuming the gamer is using all the cheat codes that let him walk through walls, fly, teleport, and perform other magical acts not available to us in the real world.

Don't get too hung up on the terminology. We're forced to use words that describe physical actions because we don't have words for equivalent mental actions.

Perhaps this sounds familiar?

Image from the "Art of Memory" treatise in Robert Fludd's Utriusque Cosmi ... Historia, Tomus Secundus, Oppenheim, 1619

❧ 16 ❦
TRAVELING

Once you've selected a Model for your memory palace, you'll need to decide how you'll travel through it in your mind. In other words, identify the Space at which you'll start, and the Space at which you plan to finish, and the winding path you'll take between those locations.

This basic fact is captured in all treatises on memory palaces, to include *Ad Herennium*, which states, "I likewise think it obligatory to have these backgrounds [Spaces] in a series, so that we never by confusion in their order be prevented from following the images [Memory Objects], proceeding from any background [Space] we wish, whatsoever its place in the series, and whether we go forwards or backwards, nor from delivering orally what has been committed to the backgrounds [Spaces]."

It will be helpful if you first decide on your direction of travel. You can think of this like floor work in a lodge. For example, I always travel in a clockwise direction. For me, that's instinctive. It is, after all, the direction in which we normally perform floor work.

But you may find a counter-clockwise direction to be more natural. Olympians run counter-clockwise in races; horses race in a counter-clockwise direction (in the U.S., anyway); NASCAR racers move counter-clockwise around racetracks. It doesn't matter which direction you choose to move in. All that matters is that you stick to one direction as much as possible.

You'll also need to decide whether you want to start from your Model's center point and move outward, or start at some outside point and move inward. I always start at an outside point and travel clockwise, spiraling in.

For example, in the third lecture of the EA degree, I start at my mailbox [an outdoor Space] and then travel counter-clockwise around my house. My second Space is my driveway, followed by the gate to my backyard, my garden, a large tree, my patio, a blueberry bush, another tree, and then another tree, and my front porch.

From that point, I spiral inside my house, starting at the garage before going through every room in my house and ending up in my basement (observe that I've combined my yard and home into a single Model, which was necessary because I needed more Spaces than either could offer individually). But I could just as easily have begun my journey in my basement and spiraled out, going through all the same locations in the opposite direction, and finishing at my mailbox.

If you are using a building with stairs connecting two or more levels, you'll need to decide whether to start at the top level and travel down, or vice versa. Most people will intuitively begin at the lowest level and move up a set of stairs only after they have exhausted all Spaces available at the lower level. You should, in this case, ensure that the last Space you reach at the lower level is adjacent to the bottom of the staircase so that your movement to the next higher level is seamless.

Staircases of sufficient size may also be used as Spaces, with, perhaps, each step being used as a Focal Point.

An alternative to starting your travel at the entry of a Space is to instead set a fixed starting point. For example, you could establish a policy of always starting your movement in the south and moving clockwise to the east. From a purely Masonic perspective, it's probably best to avoid moving a counter-clockwise direction or concluding your travel in the north. But it's ultimately your palace and your decision.

Movement Between Spaces

Movement from one outdoor space to another can, if you elect, be down in a clockwise manner, or counter-clockwise, or even in a zig-zag pattern. The pattern simply needs to be logical and intuitive.

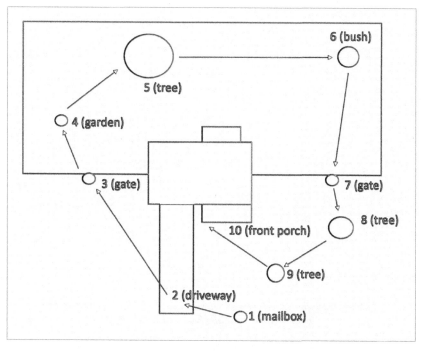

Outdoor Movement. In this illustration, ten exterior features have been selected as Spaces. Note that some potential Spaces were note used. For example, the corners of the fence surrounding the backyard and the patio at the back of the house.

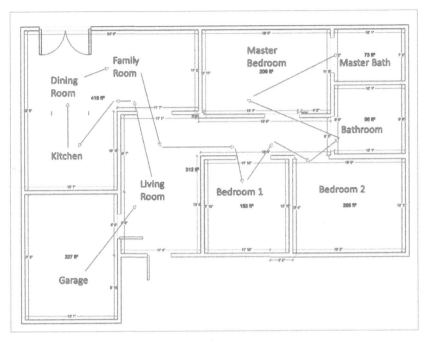

Indoor Movement. Travel through rooms of an indoor Model. Note that the hallway could have also been used as a model.

Area Movement

When you enter an Area, in which direction do you first look? I'd recommend that you look/move in the same direction as you navigate whenever possible. For example, because I move from Space to Space in a clockwise direction, when I mentally enter an indoor Space like a room, I first look left, then straight ahead, then right, then behind me. In other words, I scan the room left to right in a clockwise motion. Then I look up, to the center of the ceiling, then down, to the center of the floor, or whatever furniture, etc., might be there. That's my pattern, but it doesn't have to be yours.

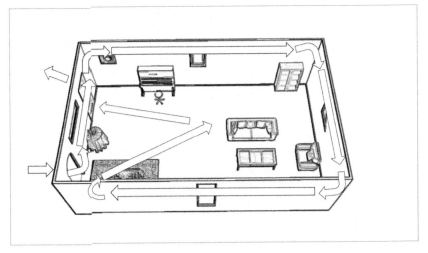

Movement through Areas. In the above example of a room used as a Space, the owner of the memory palace enters through the door at bottom left, and scans the four walls (Areas) in a clockwise direction, then the center of the room, thus using the floor as a fifth Area (four walls, plus the floor). The owner then exits this Space using the door in the upper left and moves to his next Space. He could, however, exit the same door he entered, which is frequently necessary because most rooms only have one door.

Focal Point Movement

I recommend that you initially view Focal Points from left to right because that is the direction your eyes move when reading (assuming you're reading English). When you look at, for example, a wall, assuming you've divided it into four Focal Points, you should start with the Focal Point on the left side of the wall and finish with the Focal Point on the right side of the wall.

Focal movement is, in a way, the movement of your eyes as you scan an Area. You're not moving, but your eyes are.

If you "stack" your Focal Points one atop of another, you have a few options. You could view them as you'd read sentences in a book, i.e., start at the top, and go left to right, then return to the left and go right again, and return to the left and go right again. Or you could view the left, top Focal Point, then the one below it, and only then shift right, and back to the top. I tend to cluster several Memory Objects together on stacked Focal Points, so I view Focal Points in columns, i.e., top-middle- bottom, then shift right, top-middle-bottom, and so on.

As always, do what feels comfortable for you.

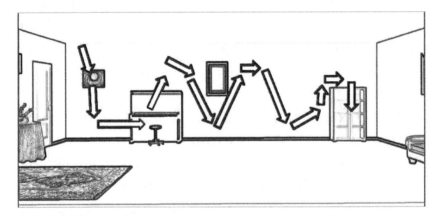

Focal Point Movement. One potential path for Focal Points, left to right, zig-zagging up and down. Use a pattern that works with your background objects and which comes naturally to you. Larger Memory Objects require more space. In this example, I am placing Memory Objects atop the photo, below it, atop the piano stool, atop the piano, left of the window, below the window, right of the window, at the bottom of the wall, left of the bookcase, atop the bookcase, and in the bookcase. When I get to the final Memory Object, I will move to the next Area in a clockwise direction.

SOLOMON'S MEMORY PALACE

Old Masonic Print. This could be viewed as a memory palace built for the purposes of list memorization, with distinct principles represented by a large number of Memory Objects which have been placed in sequence along a relatively simple, winding path in a clockwise direction. Note how the staircase directs the movement of the traveler. The creator of this palace could travel the winding path and use the Memory Objects to recall key points of a Masonic lecture, text, etc. This palace is not, however, being used for verbatim memorization, because it is clear that the Memory Objects are being used to remember concepts, not words. How many Memory Objects can you identify?

17
ESTABLISHING LANDMARKS

The establishment of Landmarks (also called anchors) in a verbatim mind palace is optional, but may be useful, and was recommended by more than one historical tutor. A Landmark is a special type of Memory Object used to help you index or partition your palace in a specific way. A Landmark is not used to remember words.

Because your memory palace uses a Model based on a real location, the size of the Spaces is pre-defined, and that size might not be a good fit for the paragraph you are storing there. That is why you will sometimes need to spread unusually large paragraphs over two Spaces, or combine two or more unusually small paragraphs into a single Space. Not doing so means either your Space will be too crowded to be effective, or you'll waste precious real estate using a large Space for a tiny paragraph.

That, in itself, is not a problem. But suppose that, for

whatever reason, you want to keep track of how the paragraphs are distributed in your model. For example, in order to pace yourself, you may want to know exactly where the midpoint of your lecture occurs, or even the quarter-points. Or maybe you want to know at what point, exactly, each topic starts and ends. Or maybe you'd like to know at what point in a lecture you need to perform an action, such as moving to a different location within the lodge, or raising an object, or making a gesture. Or maybe you'd like a way to distinguish esoteric from non-esoteric portions of what you've memorized.

To do any of the above, you'd simply place a Landmark at the needed location(s). You could place one in middle of an Area, for example, to mark the midpoint of a lecture. Or you could place one in an Area before the Memory Objects corresponding to an esoteric portion of a ritual, and another later to mark the end of that esoteric portion.

Examples of Landmarks include statues, numbers painted onto walls, obelisks, planets, and gates. Regardless of what you use, your Landmarks must be particularly striking so that they immediately come to your attention and aren't mistaken as background objects or conventional (word-based) Memory Objects. They should be very large, at least. Adding a glow, or a humming sound effect might help. A golden obelisk standing eight feet tall would work well, unless you just happen to have one of those in your home...

If your needs are simple, you can use the same Landmark several times in your memory palace. For example, if you simply want to divide your lecture into four quarters, you use the same Landmark (let's say a giant, glowing column with a number on it, i.e., 1, 2, 3, and 4), placing it in your memory palace at the correct location. Obviously, this requires that you take the time to first break the lecture into four equal parts, so that you'll know where to place the Landmarks.

If your needs are more complicated, you may wish to use Landmarks that differ from one another. For example, if your lecture addresses topics such as morality, equality, and rectitude of life, you could place a massive square, level, and plumb as Landmarks in the doorways of the related Spaces.

Again, these need to be added in some striking manner. It's not enough just to imagine a square nailed to a door. Instead, imagine a marble statue of a square that is bigger than a man and glows as brightly as the sun, or is covered in jewels, or neon lights.

Our old friend, the anonymous author of *Ad Herennium*, provides advice in this regard: "And that we may by no chance err in the number of backgrounds [Spaces], each fifth background [Space] should be marked. For example, if in the fifth we should set a golden hand, and in the tenth some acquaintance whose first name is Decimus, it will then be easy to station like marks in each successive fifth background."

The author uses a golden hand for the fifth Space because a hand has five fingers. Decimus, the Latin word for "tenth," was then a proper name, so poking a guy named "Decimus" into a room would remind you that it was the tenth Space. Today, it would be more appropriate to think of a person named "Dexter" or "Dixie."

I suspect Landmarks would have been more important two thousand years ago because the buildings and rooms of the era were not as distinct from one another as what you and I are used to. The author is recommending the use of Landmarks to avoid confusing one Space with another. That should be not a problem for the modern builder of a memory palace, but we can still use this technique for the purposes I described above, i.e., to index what we've memorized in a special manner, or to cue us to perform some action at a prescribed point in a lecture or part.

✣ 18 ✥
PLANNING YOUR MEMORY PALACE

It's important that you plan your memory palace in advance. You want the first Memory Object to be at your start point and your last Memory Object to be at your end point, and all the Memory Objects in-between logically distributed.

Here's the process:

✧

STEP 1: <u>DIVIDE YOUR MODEL INTO SPACES</u>

   a. Select your Model.

   b. Count the number of Spaces in your Model. Your goal is to have a Space for each paragraph. In other words, 10 Spaces = 10 paragraphs.

   c. If you have a published version of what you want to memorize (a book, pamphlet, cipher, monitor, etc.), use a writing instrument to draw a line under each paragraph. If a paragraph is unusually large, feel free to divide it into two paragraphs by drawing a line at logical point. If a paragraph is unusually small, don't draw a line under it, but instead include it as part of either the paragraph above or below it using brackets. These divided or combined paragraphs are the ones you'll need Spaces for.

d. Compare the number of Spaces in your Model to the number of underlined paragraphs. If you have more paragraphs than Spaces, you have two options:

#1. Find more Spaces. Could you use often-overlooked places like closets, attics, utility rooms, staircases, and hallways (indoors), or manholes, spigots, lot corners, or utility meters (outdoors)?

#2. Use a larger Space to house two paragraphs. Try to avoid this unless you have an unusually large room (usually a family room or den). If you do put two paragraphs into a room, find some background objects to use as demarcation points so you'll know where each one starts and ends. Otherwise, putting two topics in a room can result in confusion.

e. Once you have enough spaces, number each paragraph, i.e., 1, 2, 3, 4, 5...etc.

f. Decide on your path through the Spaces of your Model. Refer to the "Traveling" chapter for advice on this process. Spiral in or spiral out, or zig-zag, or use whatever method works best for you. The key is that the movement should be natural and logical. If it's erratic, without any pattern, you may not be able to remember the order of your Spaces, which is bad, because that's also the order of your paragraphs, and you don't want to get your paragraphs out of order. It might be helpful to draw out a sketch of your Model and draw arrows from one Space to the next.

SOLOMON'S MEMORY PALACE

g. Once you know the path you're going to take from one Space to another, you need to match each Space with the right paragraph. You can do this however you want. You could just jot the name of the Space in the margin of the book which contains the information you're memorizing (if you do this, I strongly recommend using a pencil!). Or you could write the paragraph number on a sketch of your Model. Or you could create an index on a separate sheet of paper. It would look something like this:

Front porch = Paragraph 1
Sidewalk = Paragraph 2
Driveway = Paragraph 3

...and so on. You might wind through your entire yard and house before finishing with, for example: Basement = Paragraph 35

STEP 2: DIVIDE YOUR SPACES INTO AREAS.

a. Count the number of sentences in each paragraph.

1) Divide unusually long sentences into two or more sentence fragments with a vertical line.

2) Combine short sentences into sentence groups by bracketing them.

For example:

The House of Representatives shall be composed of Members chosen every second Year by the People of the several States, and the Electors in each State shall have the Qualifications requisite for Electors of the most numerous Branch of the State Legislature.

(1 sentence)

- could be divided in this way:

The House of Representatives shall be composed
of Members chosen every second Year
by the People of the several States
and the Electors in each State shall
have the Qualifications requisite for Electors of
the most numerous Branch of the State Legislature
(Thus, 1 sentence becomes 6 sentence fragments, which are treated like sentences in your memory palace)

- or -

The box is brown.
Why is it brown?
The materials are unbleached.
(3 sentences)
- could be grouped in this way:
[The box is brown. Why is it brown?]
[The materials are unbleached.]
(Thus, 3 sentences become 2 sentence groups)

b. Once you've divided and grouped your sentences, write the number of sentences in the paragraph down. This is the minimum number of Areas you will need in each corresponding Space. You may assign more than one sentence to an Area if you'd like.

For example, assume that paragraph #1 contains 8 sentences and that you're using your front porch as the Space for that paragraph. This means you'll need to divide your Front Porch into 8 Areas. You could use each edge of the porch at ground level as an Area (for a total of 4), and each edge of a canopy over your porch as another 4 Areas. This gets you to 8 Areas for the 8 sentences. Another option would be two use each edge of the porch as an Area, and each corner of the porch as an Area. Use your imagination. There's always a way to make things fit.

c. Use whatever technique you like to assign the sentences in the paragraph to the Areas in the Space. Jot it down on a sketch of your Model, or create an index. This is the same process you used to tie your paragraphs to Spaces.

❦

STEP 3: DIVIDE YOUR AREAS INTO FOCAL POINTS

The only rules for Focal Points is that they should be a reasonable distance apart from one another. Traditionally, that's an arm's length, but no more than two arm's lengths. Maybe you'll need one per Area, or maybe eight. It's completely up to you how many you use and whether you put them in a line, or stack them, or a combination of both.

I would suggest not committing yourself to the number and order of your Focal Points at this point. Develop your Memory Objects for an Area first so that you'll know their sizes, and then determine which should go where. Use the background of the Area to your advantage. If your Area is, for example, a living room wall which contains a recliner, a window, and a television, you could set up your Focal Points like this:

Focal Point 1 – left of recliner

Focal Point 2 – on recliner

Focal Point 3 – right of recliner

Focal Point 4 – under or in front of the window

Focal Point 5 – under, or in front of, or on top of, the television

Again, just come up with a basic plan at this point. Wait

until you've developed your Memory Objects before deciding which to put where. Only then will you really know how many Focal Points you need in an Area.

Step 4. Create and place your Memory Objects. *Refer to Chapter 7.*

19
MOTION AND INTERACTION AS CEMENT

Motion and interaction should be used as cement to bind Memory Objects together in their proper order. One reminds you of the other and knowing what is acting on what keeps the Memory Objects in the right order. By having one Memory Object act on another Memory Object, we are using cause and effect or an anticipated sequence of events to remember the order of words in a sentence.

Putting our Memory Objects into motion is almost as important as making them strange, as noted by the author of *Ad Herennium*: "We ought, then, to set up images of a kind that can adhere longest in the memory. And we shall do so if we establish likenesses as striking as possible; if we set up images that are not many or vague, but *doing something*."

Similarly, Giambattista della Porta, in *Ars reminiscendi* ("Art of Recollection"), wrote that an image (Memory Object) was "an *animated* picture which we recall in the imagination in order to represent a fact or word."

An example might help explain what I'm talking about. Imagine I gave you five index cards. There is a single picture on each card. The pictures are:

#1: A suspicious man placing boxes of dynamite around a house

#2: A crater containing the smoldering remnants of a house

#3: A suspicious man pulling a match from a matchbook

#4: An explosion

#5: A lit fuse

If I asked you to put these cards in chronological order, you'd probably put them in this sequence: 1, 3, 5, 4, 2. I don't even have to tell you what happened. You know what happened, and you know the order of events that led to what happened: A suspicious man planted boxes of dynamite around a house, pulled a match from his pocket, lit the match, then placed the tip of the match against a fuse, and the fuse burned down until the dynamite was ignited and the house exploded. All that is left is a crater and debris.

This is an obvious sequence of events. In the same way, it's obvious to a boy that he must first put his hand into the cookie jar before he can retrieve a cookie, and that the cookie must be retrieved before it can be eaten.

Okay...so where am I going with this?

In the example above, if you flipped those cards over, you'd find that I'd written words on the back of each card:

#1: YOU

#2: PERSON

#3: ARE

#4: GREAT

#5: A

Or, in the order in which you earlier arranged them, "YOU ARE A GREAT PERSON."

Do you see what you've done? You just arranged the words on the back of the cards into a sentence without even knowing what the words were, or what the sentence was, or what word was on the back of which card. And you did that by simply placing the cards in their "natural" order, based on the pictures you saw on the front.

This is how you use motion and interaction to ensure that words are remembered in proper order. You tie words to Memory Objects and then have the Memory Objects interact in some memorable way. The chronological order in which Memory Objects interact is analogous to the chronological order in which the corresponding words appear.

You might object that I previously stated that all components of a Memory Object should be physically in contact with one another, but that Memory Objects should be an arm's length from one another to avoid confusion. Isn't having one Memory Object interacting with another defeating the purpose of that rule?

No. You first view a Memory Object by itself, and then imagine it interacting with another Memory Object. The fact that "A" is interacting with "B" shouldn't cause you to confuse A with B. They still *begin* their lives at separately. The fact that they come into contact as a result of subsequent movement shouldn't cause confusion.

❦ 20 ❦
MEMORY PALACE EXAMPLE

It's time to put what you've learned into practice. Let's use this quote from Br. Albert Pike's *Morals and Dogma*:

"Masonry is the great Peace Society of the world. Wherever it exists, it struggles to prevent international difficulties and disputes; and to bind Republics, Kingdoms, and Empires together in one great band of peace and amity. It would not so often struggle in vain, if Masons knew their power and valued their oaths."

First, break it down into sentences.

1. Masonry is the great Peace Society of the world.
2. Wherever it exists, it struggles to prevent international difficulties and disputes; and to bind Republics, Kingdoms, and Empires together in one great band of peace and amity.
3. It would not so often struggle in vain, if Masons knew their power and valued their oaths.

Sentences #2 and #3 are too long. Let's break them down into sentence fragments.

- Masonry is the great Peace Society
- of the world.
- Wherever it exists,
- it struggles to prevent
- international difficulties and disputes
- and to bind Republics,
- Kingdoms, and Empires
- together in one great band
- of peace and amity.
- It would not so often struggle in vain,
- if Masons knew their power
- and valued their oaths.

Recall that we generally use one Space for every paragraph. This example is a very short paragraph, so we'll have plenty of room to work with. Let's assume we're using a house for a Model and the family room for our Space. Because it's a small paragraph, we'll only use the walls as Areas. Assuming there are four walls, simple math (12 divided by 4) tells us that we'll be assigning three sentences (or sentence fragments, in this case) to each wall.

Thus:
Wall #1
Masonry is the great Peace Society
of the world.
Wherever it exists
Wall #2
it struggles to prevent

international difficulties and disputes
and to bind Republics
<u>Wall #3</u>
Kingdoms and Empires
together in one great band
of peace and amity
<u>Wall #4</u>
It would not so often struggle in vain,
if Masons knew their power
and valued their oaths

Because we have only three sentences per wall, we'll only need a few Focal Points. Recall that a Focal Point is any section of an Area that you can stare at or "zoom in" on.

Let's start with Wall #1, and build some Memory Objects.

Masonry is the great Peace Society
of the world
Wherever it exists...

"Masonry" is a large mason jar (the kind you'd use for canning homemade jelly). Mason jars are great Memory Objects because they are transparent. We can put other things into them, on them, or under them.

"is" is a snake, hissing.

"the" is an article, and thus optional. If you want a Memory Object for "the," you might use, as examples, a teabag or a golf tee. We'll use a tea bag as our Memory Object in this instance.

"great" = grape, or anything the color purple
"Peace" = a Peace sign
"Society" = Sew + sigh + an extraterrestrial (an "ET")
"of" = a tube of UV sunscreen
"the" = tea bag
"world" = a globe
"wherever" = this is a tough one, right? But this sounds to me a lot like "hair lever." Remember, the crazier, the better!
"it" = mitt (a kitchen mitt, catcher's mitt, or someone named "Mitt").
"exists" = two exit signs (exits = exists).

Thus, we might imagine a mason jar tipping over, then a hissing snake emerging from it. The snake slithers over a tea bag and toward a grape on the floor. The grape is next to a "peace" sign left over from a protest. On the other side of the sign, we see the hands of someone sewing. We hear a sigh and then see that the sigh came from the extraterrestrial (apparently aliens loves to sew!). The alien squirts some U.V. sunscreen lotion onto a tea bag, and then begins to rub the tea bag onto a globe of the world (this prevents global warming). On the other side of the globe is a hairy lever with a kitchen mitt impaled upon it. The thumb of the mitt points toward two exit signs on the wall.

Cycle through these images a few times in your head. It will be a clumsy exercise at first. It will be slow. But after a few repetitions, you'll find that your memory of the order of the words will catch up to your memory of the Memory Objects, and eventually the words will come to you faster than the Memory Objects, and in a few hours, days, or weeks the Memory Objects will fade into the background, only to be tapped if you find yourself forgetting the words again.

If you really want to test the effectiveness of Memory Objects in a memory palace, wait a week and then try to remember just this section of the paragraph, using the Memory Objects as your guide. I'd bet that you'll remember them and in the right order. Maybe it'll take you a few minutes of concentration, but you'll remember. However, if you merely read the words and repeated them to yourself a few times, as most people do when trying to memorize things, without using Memory Objects, odds are that within a week you'll forget them.

I'd suggest you never try to remember more than one Area a day, which means that if you were really trying to memorize this paragraph, you'd stop now, and tomorrow you'd start creating Memory Objects for your next Area.

Assuming you want to press forward, let's go to the next Area, which is the wall to the right of the wall you just used.

WALL #2:
it struggles to prevent
international difficulties and disputes
and to bind Republics

MITT ROMNEY IS "IT"

"struggles" is tough. I'm going to use two seagulls pecking at a rug. Remember, weird is good, and combining a word that starts with "s" and ends in "gulls" with the word "rug," will get the job done.

"to prevent" – I'm going to combine these two words into one Memory Object, which is a vent in the wall with a price sticker on it. The sticker has "$2" on it, but that's crossed out, and below the old price is the word, "Free." *Two-Free-Vent*. To prevent.

International – this one seems like it would be difficult, too, but all that is really required some creativity. This sounds like Enter + nat + shunnel. I'll picture an "ENTER" sign, swarming with gnats. The gnats are attracted to an open bottle of Chanel perfume that's been taped to the sign.

difficulties – a *daffy* duck in a dark robe (he's in a cult) sitting in an EZ-chair. Thus, daffy-cult-eez.

and – I sometimes picture this as a rubber band connecting the Memory Objects before and after it, or a guitar (an instrument from a *band*). On other occasions, I'll use an ant, or a hand, or sand. You might use something else entirely. I'll go with the guitar this time.

disputes - two submarines. "Das boots."

and to – I'll combine these, imagining a giant ant with a "2" painted on it.

bind – Bond. James Bond.

Republics – bananas (banana republics)

Now let's put these into motion. Mitt Romney chases two seagulls off a rug and toward a $2/Free vent. Above the vent is an ENTER sign swarming with gnats because a bottle of Chanel perfume has been taped to it. The perfume is dripping on a daffy duck (who angrily looks up). The duck is wearing a dark robe and sitting in an EZ chair. Next to the EZ chair is a guitar, which is propped on top of two model submarines. The guitar and submarines begin to move, because there is a giant ant with a "2" painted on it pushing against them. The ant bumps into James Bond, who is holding a banana in each hand, his arms crossed over his chest.

Absurd, right? But memorable. After awhile.

WALL #3:
Kingdoms and Empires
together in one great band
of peace and amity...

KINGDOMS: A KING HOLDING TWO DOME-COVERED platters, one in each hand.
    and Empires: An ant poking at a campfire
    together: Toga covered in tar
    in one: a golf ball "hole in one"
    great: a cheese grate
    band of: a bandage
    peace: a Peace sign
    and: a guitar
    amity: A book, The Amityville Horror
    A king is stumbling forward, trying to balance the domed platters in his hands. He steps on an ant sitting in front of a campfire. He then falls on a toga covered in gooey, stinky tar. A golf ball falls out of one of his pockets. It rolls to a cheese grate, which is connected to a peace sign by a Band-Aid. The peace sign topples over onto a guitar. The guitar falls over and onto the book, The Amityville Horror.

WALL #4:
It would not so often struggle in vain,
if Masons knew their power

and valued their oaths.

MITT ROMNEY IS BACK AGAIN FOR THE WORK "IT"
would not: a piece of wood with a knot in it
so often: fabric softener sheet
struggle: a straw with a gull balanced on top of it
in vain: a weather vane with an N on top
if Masons: A masonry jar with an F on it
knew their power: new hair powder
and: guitar
valued: any person named "Val" holding a Ukulele
their oaths: hair oats (yuck)

MITT ROMNEY HOLDS A KNOTTY PINE PIECE OF WOOD. He the knotty wood to push a fabric softener sheet along the floor until he is stopped by a perpendicular straw stuck in the floor. At the top of the straw is a gull. The gull, scared, flies away and over a weather vane with an N on top of it. The weather vane turns and knocks over a masonry jar with an F taped to the front of it. The jar is full of white powder, and falls over and pours the powder onto a wig. Some of the powder floats over the wig and coats a nearby guitar. The guitar is help upright by Val, who holds a Ukulele in her other hand. She drops the Ukulele into a nasty bowl of oats with a wad of hair in it.

Disgusting! But memorable.

Thus:

It would not so often struggle in vain, if Masons knew their power and valued their oaths is memorized thru images as:

Mitt wood knot soften straw gull N vane (if) Mason new hair powder and Val U'd hair oats.

THERE YOU GO. ONE PARAGRAPH DOWN. ONLY AFTER YOU memorize this paragraph should you move to the next Space (and thus your next paragraph). Remember, pace yourself. Do not try to build your entire memory palace at once.

21
PROCESS OVERVIEW

Below is a summary of the processes discussed in previous chapters.

UNDERSTAND WHAT YOU'RE MEMORIZING

- If you don't know a word, look it up. If you don't know how to pronounce a word, the internet can help you. If you don't understand the meaning of a sentence or the point of what you're memorizing, ask a brother.

ORGANIZE YOUR WORK

- Number the paragraphs.
- Combine short paragraphs (one or two sentences) into a single paragraph for numbering.

- Split up larger paragraphs into smaller paragraphs for numbering.

CREATE YOUR PALACE

- Find a Model that is an appropriate size for what you're memorizing
- Divide the Model into Spaces
- Divide the Spaces into Areas
- Divide the Areas into Focal Points (optional – you may do this later, when creating Memory Objects for that Area)

TRAVEL

- Determine the path you will take through your Model
- Determine the path you will take through each Space
- Determine the order in which you will look at Focal Points in an Area

ASSIGNMENT

- Assign paragraphs to Spaces
- Assign sentences to Areas
- Assign words to Focal Points

POPULATE YOUR PALACE WITH MEMORY OBJECTS

- Go to your first Area of your first Space and look for good Focal Points, then begin converting words to Memory Objects and placing them in or on those Focal Points. DO NOT BUILD MEMORY OBJECTS FOR THE NEXT AREA UNTIL YOU HAVE MEMORIZED THE WORDS FOR YOUR CURRENT AREA.
- Make your Memory Objects interact with one another
- Proceed to the next Area, then the next, until you have used all your Areas in that Space, then travel to the next Space. Repeat until your place is fully populated.

REINFORCEMENT

- Revisit completed Areas and Spaces as needed, even as you build new ones, in order to keep the words impressed deeply into your memory.

22

THE POWER OF OMISSION

A little-recognized but very powerful aspect of memory palaces is that they narrow your pool of options when you can't remember what a word or sentence is. In short, a memory palace tells you when a sentence or word is wrong, allowing you to quickly rule it out and seek a better alternative. Consider these variations of the example paragraph from the previous chapter:

- Masonry is a great Peace Society of the world. Wherever it exists…
- Masonry is a wonderful Peace Society. Wherever it exists…
- Masonry is the great Society of the world. Wherever it exists…
- The great Peace Society of the world is Masonry. Wherever it exists…

- Masonry is the great Peace Society of the world. Wherever it exists...
- Masonry is the great Peace Society of the world. Wherever it is found...
- Masons form the great Peace Society of the world. Where it exists...
- Wherever Masonry exists, society is peaceful.

Which one is correct? If you used the rote repetition approach to memorization, you may not be sure. They all say pretty much the same thing, just in a different way. How are you supposed to know which is the correct version?

First, let's address the issue of knowing which of these candidates contains the correct words. I think you'd agree that *great* and *wonderful* are very similar in this context. *Exists* and *is found* both seem to mean about the same thing, too, and *where* is a lot like *wherever*.

But, if you used Memory Objects to memorize this paragraph, you'd know almost immediately what are <u>not</u> the right words. You'd know that you didn't create a Memory Object for the words *wonderful* or *form* or *found*. Knowing which words are not correct is half the fight.

If you concentrate, you'll remember that there was a grape and that Memory Object must have represented a word, and in a short time, you'll remember that word is *great*.

What about those exit signs? *Exists*, right? And that terrible hair-lever? *Wherever*.

Now you just need to put the words in the right order. Perhaps: "The great Peace Society of the world is Masonry. Wherever it exists..."

No. You know that's not right because the first Memory Object was not a grape. The first Memory Object was a mason jar with a hissing snake come from it. Mason+Hiss is *Masonry is*.

Your brain excels at remembering the placement of things. Our brains had to be really, really good at that or the human species would have perished long ago. Not being able to remember where the blueberry bushes were, or the best place to hunt deer, or to find water, or where our cave was, meant death.

Remembering the exact order of words, however, was not crucial to our survival, which is why we are still pretty terrible at it. If you tried to memorize the order of words in our example without the use of Memory Objects, it would be easy for you to fool yourself into thinking that the sentence really did begin "The great Peace..." After all, that sentence has exactly the same meaning as the correct one. But getting the meaning right isn't your only goal. You want to get the words right, too, and in the right order.

23

COMPARTMENTALIZATION

A benefit of the memory palace is that it teaches you to compartmentalize what you've learned. Each Space corresponds to approximately one paragraph and each Area correlates to one or more sentences. Individuals who don't use memory palaces are often stumped if they lose their place in a lecture. For many such individuals, the lecture is one long chain of words, and forgetting even a single word can paralyze the lecturer.

But you won't have this issue. In a worst-case scenario, if you absolutely cannot remember the words corresponding to the Memory Objects in one Area of your palace, you can skip to the next Area or even the next Space. That's short of perfection, but it's a lot better than standing in the middle of the lodge like a deer in the headlights.

In fact, with a memory palace, you will literally know your lecture forward and backward. Not the words, necessarily (though you could, with some effort), but the paragraphs.

Instead of spiraling in from your starting point to your finish point, you can just reverse course.

In the third section of the Master Mason's lecture, I start at my mailbox and spiral into my house and finish in my basement. It's no problem at all starting in my basement and spiraling backward to end at my mailbox. Why should it be? I know the layout of my house and yard, and I know what paragraphs are assigned to what Spaces. You'll find that you can do the same, with practice.

You will also have the ability to start a lecture from any point between the start and finish. If a brother asks you to skip forward to a certain point in a lecture, you need only ask him what topic he wants you to start with, and then jump to the Space in your memory palace that holds that topic.

If that same brother were to say, "No, that's not it...what comes before that?", you can easily step back a Space and tell him. You can also tell him what the topic was two paragraphs before, or four, or five. It's easy. You're just walking backward through your Spaces.

But think how challenging this would be without a memory palace!

24
BEST PRACTICES

Building memory palaces is an excellent way to memorize long passages, but it should be done smartly. What follows are some memorization "best practices."

COMPREHENSION

This should go without saying, but you really need to comprehend material before you attempt to memorize it. Take long, wordy sentences and dumb them down. Much our ritual was written long ago by well-meaning brothers who were apparently getting paid by the word (and perhaps a bonus for obscure words or words with five or more syllables).

One technique I've found effective is to give a title to each paragraph. If you can't come up with a title, odds are you don't really understand the paragraph. Once you have each paragraph titled, review the titles and you may see the "big picture," i.e., what the author was trying to convey, and how.

Find the meaning of words you don't know, and be sure you know how to pronounce them. If a word seems familiar but is used in a weird way, look it up. Try to determine how the word was used when the ritual was written. It might be very different than how the word is used today.

Take, for example, the word "dispose." Today, we normally connect this word with another word: disposal. We are asked to properly dispose of our recyclables and used oil and trash. Disposing of something has thus come to mean "getting rid of it."

Yet this wasn't the original meaning. The word's origin is the Latin word *disponere*, which meant "to arrange." In old French, this became *poser*, which meant, "to place." Have you ever been *posed* for a photograph by a photographer?

Taken together, we can assume that a century ago dispose meant "to place or arrange" and not "to get rid of or throw away." This is important. In this sense, disposing means to "move someone or something to another location."

Now, think about that. If *you* are being disposed in lodge, you're probably being sent from one location to another. It follows that if you're not being moved from one location to another, you're not being disposed. And, if you're standing in place, you haven't been disposed.

Related to this, in ye olden times, *conduct* meant "to guide." Thus, if you were disposed (instructed to move from one location to another), and didn't know how to get there, you would probably be conducted there by someone else.

Consequently, we'd expect the words *disposed* and *conducted* to be paired. One should follow the other. If I had memorized a sentence that contained the word *disposed*, I'd anticipate that next sentence might contain the word *conducted*. If I thought a sentence contained the word *conducted*, but the previous sentence didn't contain the word *disposed*, I'd have a reason to doubt my memory and to think a moment longer about what I was about to say.

ANALYSIS

Here are some things to look for when studying a part, lecture, etc.:

Patterns. Trust me, they're there. Once you find the patterns, you'll understand the "rhythm" of what you're memorizing, which can be a tremendous help in memorizing the text.

Anchors. For example, if the word "then" is used four times in a paragraph, you can make "then" an anchor, i.e., either the start or end of a series of Memory Objects. That will mentally cue you to start the next series.

Pairs. The rituals use a lot of paired words. These words are usually synonymous, or nearly so. For example, "here and in this place," or "secret and unseen," or "forbidden and not permitted." There are reasons for this, none of which can be discussed here, but zooming in on these word pairs can be useful. Often, they will reveal a pattern. Try to come up with a single Memory Object for paired words like these.

CHUNKING

Chunking is the division of what you're trying to memorize into bite-size portions. Never bite off more than you can chew, and never overtask yourself by trying to memorize too much at once. Memorization is a gradual process. Overwhelming yourself will result in failure, and failure will result in discouragement, and that could cause you to give up on memorization altogether.

Per *Ad Herennium*, "If a speech is on the long, learn it in fragments." It was solid advice two thousand years ago, and it's solid advice today.

I'd suggest you start with the goal of learning one sentence a day and becoming familiar with the following sentence. You might find this too easy, in which case you should up your game and memorize two sentences a day. If that's too tough, just go for a few words a day. This isn't a race. Do what works best for you. The stuff you're trying to memorize has been around for a long, long time. It's not going anywhere.

And remember, by "sentence" I'm referring to both regular sentences *and* sentence fragments, which shouldn't be any longer than about ten words, or any shorter than about five. Memorizing a two-word sentence isn't much of an effort, after all, while memorizing a sentence with hundred words is over-doing it.

Put in terms of your memory palace, you should try to memorize perhaps an Area a day.

STUDY INTERVALS

This is important. You must take a systematic approach to memorization, and that approach needs to include what is known as "spaced repetition." This is also referred to as "spaced retrieval," or "graduated intervals," or "spaced rehearsal."

Think of your brain as a muscle. If you've had any experience with weightlifting, you know that working the same muscles every day, or several times a day, will actually retard muscle growth. Muscles need time to recuperate after a workout, with the larger muscles needing more time than the smaller ones.

Consequently, serious weightlifters maintain a schedule. They might exercise their biceps every three days, for example, that interval being just long enough to allow the muscles to reach maximum growth before again stressing them in hopes of gaining still more growth.

The brain works in much the same way. Memorization, like weightlifting, is best accomplished through interval training.

In memorization, we don't focus on the size of the muscle. We focus on how well we've memorized something. Those things which we have memorized best – perhaps the first two sentences of a paragraph – should be studied less often than those things we've memorized least - perhaps the third and fourth sentences of the same paragraph.

Here, many of you are nodding your heads and mumbling, "Of course. Why should I waste time studying what I've already memorized? It only makes sense to study the portions of a lecture or part which I haven't memorized. I don't need you to tell me that!"

And you're right. The thing is, many of us do continue to study what we've already memorized, in addition to those things we haven't memorized, or haven't fully memorized. We do this thinking that the more we study everything, the better off we'll be. We assume that studying the same sentence every day, even if we've already memorized it, is better than studying it every few days, or every few weeks. Doesn't constantly studying the same sentence, again and again, really hammer that sentence into our brains? Isn't that a good thing, even if it might seem like a waste of time?

No. In fact, that's a bad thing. You're actually hurting yourself – or at least, your memory.

Here's the deal:

When you first memorize a sentence, it is not in your long-term memory. It is in your short-term memory. By definition, your short-term memory is reliable for only a short period of time. You want what you've memorized to be stored in your long-term memory. Your short-term memory is only capable of holding a relatively small amount of information, on a temporary basis, while your long-term memory can hold a massive amount of information with almost no effort for a much longer period.

So, how do we get that sentence you memorized from short-term memory to long-term memory? By letting the brain do it naturally. By studying something at prescribed intervals, you are "telling" your brain that the thing you are memorizing isn't going away. It's going to keep appearing, again and again, for an indefinite period of time. The brain, which is highly efficient, will salute smartly and begin moving that thing from "temporary holding" – your short-term memory – into the long-term memory, or "permanent storage."

But if you study something you already know, too frequently, your brain won't put it into long-term memory. It will remain in short-term memory. Movement of anything remembered from short-term memory to long-term memory only happens if you ignore it for a prescribed period, and then reintroduce it, and then ignore it again for an even longer period, then reintroduce it, and so on.

Here's an analogy: If you can get any food you want, whenever you want, from your local grocery store, there's no reason for you to store food in your home. But if there is an economic depression, or a war, you might find that your grocery store is often out of the things you need for days, weeks, or even months. Under such circumstances, you would not rely on your grocery store (your "short-term" supplier), but would instead buy as many food necessities as you could afford when they were available, and then you'd store them away for future use ("long-term storage").

Your brain works in a similar manner. You need to toughen it up and say, "Look, I'm not going to keep going over this same sentence every day, because, honestly, it's making you lazy. I'm going to deprive you of it for a while, and then test you, and you better be ready when that happens."

How do you know when it's time to stop studying something, and how long do you wait before your return to it to test yourself?

The easiest approach is to use computer software or a mobile device app. You can find these via an internet search for "flashcard software" or "flashcard app," or by just going to the Wikipedia page for one of these terms and scrolling down a few paragraphs.

The programs and apps typically use virtual flashcards. After quizzing you on something you're trying to memorize, they'll ask you a question such as "How difficult was it to get the answer right?" It will offer you a choice of answers like "easy," "a little difficult," "difficult," and "impossible."

If you so you click on "easy," the program won't show you

the card again for a period of time – it could be hours, days, or weeks. If you select "a little difficult," the interval will be shorter. If you select "impossible," you'll probably see that question again within minutes or even seconds (the program assumes that if you've taken the time to study before continuing the quiz).

You may wonder how you can use software or an app with esoteric materials. After all, the program has to know what to ask you, right? Doesn't that mean you have to type the esoteric materials into the program?

No. Remember, you're building a memory palace. The "front" of the virtual flashcard, which is the "question," can be "Kitchen, wall with sink," or "Backyard, garden," or "Living Room, center." The "back" of the flashcard, which is the correct "answer," can be a list of one or more of your Memory Objects – however many it takes to remind you of the right words (be cautious here – don't make the answer obvious to anyone, including non-Masons, or Masons of lower degrees).

You don't actually record the words themselves. If you are so utterly stumped that even your Memory Objects don't give you the right words, it's time for you to refer back to your cipher, or monitor, or another brother.

Using our "Peace Society" example, for flashcard #1, I would enter the following information into the program:

FRONT OF FLASHCARD (THE "QUESTION"): LIVING ROOM, Wall #1

Back of the flashcard (the "answer"): Jar – Snake – Grape – Sign – Alien – Globe – Hair – Lever – Exit Signs

. . .

IF YOU'RE THE OLD-FASHIONED TYPE AND WOULD RATHER use real flashcards, you should investigate the *Leitner System*. There are plenty of websites and videos that can teach you how to organize your flashcards into separate piles or boxes to help you space your studies. If you want to go completely retro, you can probably find a book on that subject at your local library.

REVISIT THE SOURCE MATERIAL

While it's a great achievement to reach a point at which you think you've memorized everything you need to memorize, it pays to revisit your source material before you get overly confident. I once thought that I had a lecture memorized forward and backward, only to discover that I had dropped a Memory Object somewhere along the way. I never noticed, and no one else did either, because no one else knew the lecture and because what I said still made perfect sense. It just wasn't correct.

It wasn't until I scanned the lecture (after having given it twice!) that I saw what I had been omitting. Inserting or correcting words into something you've memorized gets more difficult with the passing of time. Better to check your memory against the source sooner than later - and again, on occasion.

MEDITATION

Meditation means different things to different people. For me, meditation is sitting on my couch with my eyes closed, a cup of coffee close at hand. For some, it's staring at the horizon. For others, it's sitting cross-legged with an erect posture. In whatever form, the purpose of meditation is to shove aside all the daily clutter that weighs your mind down in order to focus on something more important – or to not focus on anything at all.

In addition to being a stress reliever, meditation helps you memorize. It's important that you find some time and place each day to take a leisurely stroll through your memory palace, taking note of missing or difficult Memory Objects and ensuring you can travel through it without getting lost or confused. Missing Memory Objects are an indication that you might need to find alternatives to what you initially created. Forgetting how to move from one Space to another suggests you need to find a more intuitive route through your palace.

A fantastic book on meditation in a Masonic context is *Contemplative Masonry*, by C.R. Dunning, Jr. Its subtitle is *Basic applications of mindfulness, meditation, and imagery for the craft*.

TESTING

It's important that you not rely on study alone to memorize a work. You need to test yourself, or better, have someone else test you. This test could take one of several forms. Perhaps it's just you reciting what you've memorized and being corrected by another brother, as needed. Perhaps it's a brother challenging you to recite a portion of a work without the portion preceding it. It could be another person giving you different variations of a work and asking you which is right. As always, use your imagination.

The need for testing has been proven to help retain those

things memorized. Reference Roediger and Karpicke's study, *Test-enhanced learning: taking memory tests improves long-term retention*, which reads, "Taking a memory test not only assesses what one knows, but also enhances later retention, a phenomenon known as the testing effect. We studied this effect with educationally relevant materials and investigated whether testing facilitates learning only because tests offer an opportunity to restudy material. In two experiments, students studied prose passages and took one or three immediate free-recall tests, without feedback, or restudied the material the same number of times as the students who received tests. Students then took a final retention test 5 min, 2 days, or 1 week later. When the final test was given after 5 min, repeated studying improved recall relative to repeated testing. However, on the delayed tests, prior testing produced substantially greater retention than studying, even though repeated studying increased students' confidence in their ability to remember the material. *Testing is a powerful means of improving learning, not just assessing it.*" (italics are mine).

While you should test yourself using the interval study system earlier discussed, self-testing isn't enough. You need someone else to test you. That's the type of testing the study focused on. For you, this means finding a brother to test you, i.e., listen to you recite what you've memorized and correct you or offer help, as necessary. This should be a brother who has already memorized what you're studying on, or who can refer to a monitor or cipher and follow along.

That said, you should advise the person testing you only to intervene if you've made a mistake or asked him for help. There will be times when you simply need a second to collect your thoughts. Pauses are not errors.

STUDY TIMES

Finding time to study or mentally rehearse what you've memorized isn't easy. I've found that mental rehearsal (going over what I've memorized in my head) is easiest during my drive to and from work, and when I go to bed. Everyone's got a different schedule, of course. If there's a time of the day in which you're restricted from doing much of anything else, that's a good time to mentally go over what you've memorized.

I sometimes arrive early on lodge nights and go over my memorized parts while still in my car. Lunchtime can also afford you a good opportunity to study. Whatever your situation, the important thing is that you find time to spend a few minutes each day to study. If you can memorize just a few words in that short span of time, that's a success. Be mindful of the twenty-four-inch gauge, and manage your time wisely.

PRINCIPLES OF OUR CRAFT

- The beehive: Be industrious. Study every day.
- The hourglass: Time flies. Don't put it off.
- The ladder: Have faith in your abilities, hope to achieve great things, and help your brothers with memorization, even as they help you.
- The all-seeing eye: Think about what you're reading, why it's important, and the historical or philosophical significance of it.
- The anchor: Find memory anchors in your memory locations.

- The mosaic pavement: Be methodological. Look for patterns. Be thankful for what you've learned and use your successes as foundations for greater things.
- The sword pointing to a naked heart: Keep in mind that you will be rewarded according to your merits (efforts).
- The book of constitutions guarded by the Tyler's sword: Remember not to disclose esoteric portions to those standing before the porch.
- Compass: Don't over-extend yourself.
- 24" gauge: Budget your time and pace yourself. Plan ahead and know how many lines you'll need to learn each day to reach your goal.

25
MAINTENANCE

You need to establish some kind of maintenance schedule, especially if you're not using what you've memorized on a regular basis. I attempt to recite the parts I've memorized at least once every two weeks. It's not difficult and doesn't take much time. It's certainly easier than forgetting what you've memorized and starting over!

No matter how well you've memorized your work, you're going to forget things. This is particularly true if what you've memorized is needed only periodically. As an example, one of my roles is to recite the third section of the EA degree lecture. Like most lodges, mine doesn't need to perform this degree every month. In fact, three or four months might pass between EA degrees. While I do occasionally rehearse my lecture, there's no substitute for performing it live. Unattended, a memory palace can slowly start to crumble, which means you're going to have to do some upkeep from time to time.

When doing maintenance, don't feel compelled to stick to your original plan. As I mentioned earlier, the inability to recall a Memory Object probably means that it wasn't a very good one. If milk turns sour, you don't put it back in the refrigerator in hopes that it'll improve the next day. You throw it away and buy fresh milk.

Memory palaces work the same way. If a Memory Object repeatedly fails you, don't force the issue. Instead, consider replacing it. Look for something better to patch the hole you've found. That might require you to replace the one object, or it might require you to replace several objects, or even redesign an Area or Space. Don't panic. That's natural. Patching is a part of the process.

Once you've completed your memory palace and have memorized what you want to memorize, the Memory Objects will probably begin to recede. They'll pop back into existence on occasion, usually if you struggle with a word, but my experience is that they eventually recede so far back that it can be difficult to find them again. This isn't a bad thing. As already discussed, the Memory Objects are molds, and are, in a way, broken and discarded when not needed (at least with verbatim memorization). You can always create new ones or bring the old ones back to life, if necessary.

Interestingly, the Model is permanent, or nearly so. Long after the Memory Objects are discarded, the Model remains, like an ancient theater devoid of actors or props. This means that you'll probably find yourself mentally wandering it when reciting what you've memorized, even when the Memory Objects are missing. I assume this is because neural pathways used for spatial relationships differ substantially for those used for Memory Objects.

Models, once built, are almost impossible to destroy. This is a good thing because the Models are still effective at helping us retain what we've memorized even without its Memory Objects. Stepping into a room, glancing at a wall, or surveying background objects is usually all that's necessary for the "ghosts" of the Memory Objects to do their work. The words will come to you.

When you reach this point, you may opt to transform your memory palace from a verbatim Model to a list Model. This is simple enough. Simply build a single Memory Object for each Space and place it in a conspicuous place, like a doorway. If the Space houses a paragraph on the jewels of the lodge, for example, simply place the jewels of the lodge there. If the paragraph is about the morality, place a large Square there. I think of these Memory Objects as "markers." They help you keep your house in order.

And here is something that merits contemplation: Within Freemasonry, almost all of the markers you'll need already exist in the form of symbols, emblems, hieroglyphs, etc. You don't have to create them. You simply need to take the things already provided you and put them in the right place. Doing that can lead to an epiphany – several, even.

But those should be experienced, not described.

26
SUPPLEMENTARY TECHNIQUES

While I believe that the memory palace is the best technique for most brothers to memorize long passages, there are other techniques which can be used either alone, or as supplements, to the memory palace.

DRAW YOUR MEMORY OBJECTS

Studies show that drawing things helps us to remember them. Drawing your Memory Objects would thus be a great way of impressing them more deeply into your mind. You might even draw multiple Memory Objects to cement their relationship to one another in an Area or Space. You don't need to be an artist. The drawings might be horrible, but it doesn't matter. You're not putting them on display. You're drawing to enhance your memory.

It could be objected that drawing Memory Objects of

esoteric portions of our craft is a violation of our oaths. I think that's a stretch. First, it assumes that you're one heck of an artist. Second, it assumes that someone who sees your drawings of Memory Objects could somehow decipher them. Given the abstract nature of Memory Objects and the dozens of ways they might be formed, this seems highly unlikely. Unless the objects can be made intelligible by others, you have not broken your oath. Use your own discretion.

TRIGGERING

Have you ever eaten a food that you haven't eaten in years and almost immediately experienced a flood of memories from that previous period? Somehow the flavor seems to cause long-dormant neurons in your brain to spark back to life, causing you to think about people and events that you've not thought about for years. It doesn't have to be the taste of food or drinks, though. The trigger could be a scent or sound that you've not experienced for a long time.

Like so many things, you can use this to your advantage. When studying something you want to memorize, try chewing a type of gum that you're not used to. The more exotic, the better. Only use that gum on one of two occasions: during study, and during recital in lodge. You could use a mint instead of gum if you can't restrain yourself from chewing, which is just bad manners if you're speaking to brothers or an initiate in lodge assembled.

Another option is to use a diffuser or room freshener with an unusual scent when studying. Prior to lodge, place a tiny amount of that scent on a handkerchief and take a whiff of it just before reciting what you've memorized. Easy does it, though. You don't want to turn yourself into a walking stick of deodorant.

Incidentally, the smell of rosemary while studying has been shown to significantly increase memory retention – some studies show an increase of up to 75%. Do a search on the internet for more information.

WORD DOODLING (NON-ESOTERIC ONLY)

This technique works best if you have a computer with some kind of text editing program, which most of you do. Often times you can find non-esoteric portions of ritual and lectures on the internet. Be mindful of the fact that such passages might still be considered esoteric in your jurisdiction, however, in which case your oath would arguably prohibit you from copying and pasting them into word processing program. But assuming the words you want to memorize are not esoteric, you can copy and paste them into a text document, or else type them in, perhaps referring to your monitor.

Once you have the words in a text document, your task is simply to move the words around, perhaps randomly at first, in search of patterns. To illustrate what I'm talking about, I'll again use this excerpt from Morals and Dogma:

"Masonry is the great Peace Society of the world. Wherever it exists, it struggles to prevent international difficulties and disputes; and to bind Republics, Kingdoms, and Empires together in one great band of peace and amity. It would not so often struggle in vain, if Masons knew their power and valued their oaths."

First, try to form up the paragraph into the most perfect square you can. After a few tries, here's what I came up with:

> *Masonry is the great Peace Society of the world. Wherever it exists, it struggles to prevent international difficulties and disputes; and to bind Republics, Kingdoms, and Empires together in one great band of peace and amity. It would not so often struggle in vain, if Masons knew their power and valued their oaths.*

But I can do better than that, right?

> *Masonry is the great Peace Society of the world. Wherever it exists, it struggles to prevent international difficulties and disputes; and to bind Republics, Kingdoms, and Empires together in one great band of peace and amity. It would not so often struggle in vain, if Masons knew their power and valued their oaths.*

Which later became:

> *Masonry is the great Peace Society of the world. Wherever it exists, it struggles to prevent international difficulties and disputes; and to bind Republics, Kingdoms, and Empires together in one great band of peace and amity. It would not so often struggle in vain, if Masons knew*

SOLOMON'S MEMORY PALACE

their power and valued their oaths.

Hmmm...this is tough.

> *Masonry is the great Peace Society*
> *of the world. Wherever it exists, it*
> *struggles to prevent international dif-*
> *ficulties and disputes; and to bind Re-*
> *publics, Kingdoms, and Empires togeth-*
> *er in one great band of peace and amity.*
> *It would not so often struggle in vain, if*
> *Masons knew their power and valued*
> *their oaths.*

Still not there. But I never will be, honestly, and neither will you. These words were not designed to be organized into a perfect square. But by acting on the words, i.e., by moving them around and trying to form them into a shape, you're impressing them into your mind. The mind loves puzzles, and you've turned this paragraph into a puzzle.

Here's a second exercise, in which I edit the paragraph until every line ends in a two-letter word:

> *Masonry is*
> *the great Peace Society of*
> *the world. Wherever it*
> *exists, it*
> *struggles to*
> *prevent international difficulties and disputes and to*
> *bind Republics, Kingdoms, and Empires together in*
> *one great band of*

> *peace and amity. It*
> *would not so*
> *often struggle in*
> *vain, if*
> *Masons knew their power and valued their oaths.*

Here I've formed the words into a half-pyramid (after several attempts):

> *Masonry*
> *is the great*
> *Peace Society of*
> *the world. Wherever*
> *it exists, it struggles to*
> *prevent international difficulties*
> *and disputes and to bind Republics,*
> *Kingdoms, and Empires together in one great*
> *band of peace and amity. It would not so often struggle*
> *in vain, if Masons knew their power and valued their*
>   *oaths.*

The variations are almost limitless. You can divide the paragraph into segments beginning or ending with the word "the" or "it" or "to," for example. Use your imagination. Remember, there is no wrong or right way to do this. This is a bit like doodling on a piece of paper. You're just allowing your mind to play around with the words in a freeform manner, but in doing so, you'll be unconsciously creating a register of the words, and their relationship with one another, in your brain.

IDEOPHONES

Have you heard of the Bouba/Kiki Effect?
    Take a look at these two images:

BOB W. LINGERFELT

Assume that one of these shapes is named *Bouba*. The other is *Kiki*. Say those names out loud. Which one do you think is Kiki? Which one is Bouba? It's not a trick question. You don't have to meditate on it. Just go with your gut.

Stop reading until you make your guess.

Got it?

Okay...

If you're like most of the human race, you guessed that the figure on the left is Kiki, and the one on the right is Bouba. Why?

Well, it's complicated (isn't everything?), but the bottom line is that our brains have a peculiar way of connecting sounds with shapes – regardless of the language we speak. This test, and a similar one using the words *Takete* and *Maluma*, has been posed to speakers of Spanish, English, and Tamil, and the results were consistent (as you might guess, Takete was overwhelming associated with the figure that looks like a deformed throwing star).

This is an example of what is called *sound symbolism*, which is the theory that some sounds have specific primal meanings. The words, which evoke a vivid impression of an idea (such as a sound, color, smell or emotion) are called idiophones. It's a fascinating phenomenon and there's a lot of debate about why this happens. Our brains can link images and shapes (and thus Memory Objects) to words and ideas in some very weird ways.

A take-away from this is this: If you find that a word reminds you of a shape, color, or anything else, or vice versa, don't ignore the connection simply because you don't understand it. The fact that it exists at all means it is somehow hardwired in your brain, and those types of connections are very powerful. Use them.

27
SOME CLOSING THOUGHTS

As I stated at the beginning of this book, in learning *verbatim* memorization you have also learned *list* memorization.

Because verbatim memorization is used to memorize long strings of words, it is less "elegant" than its simpler cousin. The Memory Objects created to help you remember words are usually weird or comical or abstract and they usually have nothing to do with the ideas represented by the words. There is rarely a correlation between the odd collection of things we jumble together to remember a word and what the word represents.

List memorization *can* be like that but it doesn't have to be. A single Memory Object like the sun can have a powerful connection to whatever concepts a Space holds (justice, enlightenment, fertility, etc.). Though the memory palaces required for Masonic lectures and parts are necessarily of the verbatim varieties, almost all Masonic symbols, emblems, etc.

are designed to teach or remind us of ideas and concepts, not words. The temples, lodge rooms, fields and hills in old Masonic illustrations bear a striking resemblance to memory palaces of the list variety. The appearance of a square, level, or broken column, serves not to remind us of words but of something bigger. Perhaps something not fully describable by words.

While the Memory Objects used for verbatim memorization differ considerably from those used for list memorization, the Models used by both techniques are almost identical. The Models are selected, constructed, and navigated in much the same way regardless of the type of memorization you're pursuing. True, a verbatim Model is more crowded, and its Memory Objects have less significance, but otherwise it is the same as a Model used for list memorization.

The perks of knowing how to construct a memory palace extend beyond enhanced memory. A palace builder can more easily discern the tell-tale signs of memory palaces which have been concealed in art, literature, religious texts, music, and plays. You may even be able to determine how and why they were built. Who knows what light might be found within the walls of those hidden palaces?

Happy hunting.

A THOUSAND YEARS AFTER MEMORY PALACES WERE described in *Ad Herennium*, they were still being used memorization. But during the Renaissance, memory palaces were transformed into something far more complex. This transformation was largely the result of theologians, philosophers and hermeticists who began to speculate that the mind was equipped, or perhaps designed, to mirror the reality outside of it – or vice versa. This meant that we were no longer restricted to learning about reality through our senses alone. We could polish our minds and look deeper inside its recesses to find truths that our senses were unable to detect.

Such individuals believed that, because man is made in the image of God, the human mind comes equipped with a built-in blueprint for the entire universe. Well, more than the universe, really. We're talking about a blueprint for everything. Reality itself.

As might be expected, this concept further evolved into the theory that those who fully comprehend reality must also be able to shape it. If the mind and reality are cut from the same cloth and can be made to align with one another, mind and reality should be on an even playing field. If the mind can be affected by things "outside" of it, shouldn't the mind be equally capable of affecting *those things*?

But how to make that happen? Today, most adherents to this theory, or one like it, would say that it is accomplished through pure force of will, or daily confirmations, or imagining something with such force that the universe is forced to take a knee and give you what you want.

These strategies were, however, alien to Renaissance practitioners of *mystical* memory palaces. They lived in an age of religious fervor and magic. If you wanted the universe or any other power to bend to your will, you had to work for it. One approach was to reverse-engineer memory palaces. If a palace could be used to record in the mind things which are observed through the senses, couldn't a palace be carefully constructed and populated with Memory Objects that caused

– one might say "tricked" – the universe into "remembering" them, and thus causing them to pop into existence?

Large books with far more details are available on this topic, several of which I have already cited. There were many thoughts on how a memory palace might be used actively instead of passively. I introduce this topic only because I think it appropriate that a book that teaches the memory palace technique, and which is written primarily for Freemasons, should provide at least a cursory overview of how it was used by a select few in the era which gave birth to the speculative, organized iteration of our craft.

YOU MAY FIND, AS I HAVE, THAT THE CONSTRUCTION OF memory palaces is somewhat addictive. Not in a bad way. It's just that once you've built one or two, your brain may seem a bit anxious to find another target. The creation process is stimulating – rather like solving a puzzle. There are people who love crossword puzzles and can't let a morning pass without attempting one. Memory palaces can have the same effect.

You will probably find that your overall memory increases, even when you aren't using the memory palace technique. As discussed earlier in this book, the construction of palaces appears to rewire a person's brain and make it more efficient. I'll leave it to the researchers to explain why this happens, but I think we can all agree that's it's a good thing.

Since I began creating memory palaces, I've come to ponder what it means to create a Memory Object. I mean, yes, it sounds straight-forward. I've even explained how to do it. But I've become increasingly aware that there is nothing in my head — or yours, or anyone else's — *other than* Memory Objects.

We're all minds stuck in some invisible world with our ethereal hands behind our ethereal backs, pacing ethereal floors with our ethereal legs, waiting impatiently for one of the senses to detect some kind of external activity and report back to us. We are a few degrees removed from whatever it is on the other side of our senses. We've got no idea what is really out there. The senses are simultaneously gates and barriers, and our understanding of what lies beyond "the wall" is based solely on cryptic symbols handed us by five unreliable messengers.

I now understand why our craft focuses, in part, on the five senses. Previously, I'd considered the lectures on the senses somewhat boring. After all, the senses are physical. Biological. There's nothing esoteric about them. Smell is...well, smell. How does one obtain "light" from smell? It all seemed rather silly.

Yet if one understands that the senses are the gates between two realities, and that the messengers who man those gates are responsible for forming our perception of what lies beyond the walls, their importance is obvious.

My point is only that memory palaces are nothing new. Ultimately, *our reality is a memory palace*. Building them is something we've been doing since we were first gifted the spark of consciousness. It's something we're doing even now. This very moment.

As Freemasons, we should be mindful of the grand, omnipresent palaces in which we truly reside. We are kings trapped in the middle chamber of our own castles. We rely on our senses to sketch images of the vast country beyond our castle walls which we cannot directly experience. We stare in confusion at the shadows cast on the interior walls of our castles by the blinding light that resides at their centers. We compare the shadows to the sketches of our senses and construct little models that we hope somehow capture the essence of what none of us can truly see. These models are the Memory Objects of our minds and souls.

You have seen the effort and care required to build a memory palace dedicated to a single topic, such as a lecture. Shouldn't we be equally methodical and tireless in the perpetual construction of that grand memory palace which we imagine is our reality?

HISTORICALLY, THE AMOUNT OF MEMORIZATION REQUIRED for Masons to achieve proficiency in the degrees has been daunting - arguably far more than necessary to perpetuate the rites and purported secrets of the craft. It is for this reason that I suspect memorization was ultimately an end unto itself, i.e., the memory trials of Masons seeking degrees were designed to produce the kind of man that has always been prized in Freemasonry - the *thinking* man.

Consequently, the reduced memorization requirements of recent decades may have been more detrimental to the science of Freemasonry than we suspect. Common wisdom is that this retreat was necessary to maintain or increase membership. But I think the retreat was also caused by a perception that we were not practicing the equality we so often espouse. After all, we are all born with different gifts.

Memory might be one of them, or it might not be. Why should we disqualify men with other valuable talents simply because they aren't good at memorization, particularly if those men have met all other prerequisites and are enthusiastic about the craft?

It's a good question. But I think it misses the point. The objective of Freemasonry is to make men better, and that is done in degrees. It isn't necessary that a candidate be able to achieve the degree of Master Mason when he first appears in lodge, nor is he expected to achieve any degree without the help of a mentor.

The collapse of the degree structure, at least in the United States, is one reason we have reduced the once rigorous memory standards of our forefathers. There are few permanent Entered Apprentice or Fellowcraft lodges within our country. There simply aren't enough new members to support them as independent institutions. Consequently, business meetings and many other activities are open only to Master Masons. Not wanting to leave any brother outside the door (both for fear he might wander away and because our sense of justice and equality forbids it) we have elected to get everyone inside as quickly as possible.

Where might this lead us?

Imagine it is the year 2050. In your town there is a venerable old college which has taught traditional subjects (science, literature, mathematics, etc.) for two centuries, and which offers a four-year degree in a variety of fields. Despite the pedigree of the alumni produced by the college, young people no longer see a need to be taught how to read, write, or perform mathematical computations, because computers can perform that work for them. The only reason students come to our college is that they want the degree for what it represents (at least, in theory), and they want the "college experience," which primarily consists of extracurricular events.

But, over time, the allure of the degree and the extracurricular activities aren't enough to maintain enrollment. Each year there are a dwindling number of students. This concerns the college board because there are still many students who truly want to come to their college to learn, but the college isn't sustainable without those other students who come to the school for the fancy-looking degree and the extracurricular activities.

The college board takes two steps. First, it increases and promotes its extracurricular offerings. Second, it reduces the required period for a "four-year degree" to three years, which has the ostensibly-positive effect of increasing the number of students in each classroom and makes the college look healthier than it really is.

Yet, attendance continues to dwindle. There remain a few students who truly want to learn the old and largely forgotten sciences, and who do not wish to depend on computers to do their thinking for them, but there's not enough to keep the college viable. So, the board again increases its extracurricular activities and again reduces the time it takes to get a four-year degree, this time to two years. The hollowed classrooms are again full.

Note, however, that up till now, the academic requirements to obtain a degree have remained the same. Though a student can get a "four-year" degree in two years, there has been no reduction in what must be learned. Students still have to know their stuff to graduate. This means the climb is shorter but the hill is much steeper. What could once be learned in a year must now be learned in six months!

Those students attending college to *learn* grumble a bit but march on.

Those students who are not there to learn grumble much louder and complain that the academic standards are too tough. No person, they argue, should reasonably be expected to learn in two years what was once learned in four! They begin to drop out.

Again, the college is faced with dwindling attendance. The board feels compelled to reduce the educational requirements for a four-year degree into a *single year*. If not, it will cease to exist, and how would that be fair to those few students who are present to learn?

Each three-month period is now rated as the equivalent of a "traditional" year, which means that a student who was a Freshman in September will be a Sophomore in December, a Junior by March, and a Senior by June.

In this way the board feels that the students are still getting the "college experience" they yearn for. They still have an opportunity to wear school rings and hats, can participate in extracurricular activities, and get to proclaim themselves college graduates when all is said and done.

The problem is that darn learning curve. Is it really fair to expect even the academically-minded students to compress four years of learning into one year?

No. It might not even be possible.

The solution? You have surely guessed it by now. Reduce the academic requirements.

The results are equally predictable. Attendance by those who don't really care to learn increases…for a while. But attendance by those who came to the college to learn evaporates. After all, the college doesn't really have much to offer those students except a musty old library and its famous history. That's not going to be enough. And with the loss of those students, the college soon loses its ability to teach. What value is there in teaching if no one present wants to learn?

The college becomes a shell of its former self. Desperate, the board decides to convert the former academic institution to a social club, filling its former classrooms with hologram machines, restaurants, meditation labs, or whatever else the public fancies. But other dying institutions are doing that, too. What makes the college unique? Only its history. And that ultimately won't be enough.

In the end, collapsing the four-year degree program into a single year and then reducing the learning requirements to almost nothing didn't save the college. At best, it bought it some time.

The experiences of this college are mirrored by every academic institution in the world. Even as the old-timers bemoan the loss of these venerable institutions, they fail to recognize the loss of something more important.

Everything that the college once taught.

In the years that follow, anything that can be known by a computer is forgotten by man. Mathematics becomes an arcane art. Reading and writing are widely viewed as some primitive form of magic. Thinking is viewed with suspicion – why should we frail humans think when all the wisdom of the world is contained in the atomic memory of the newest computers?

Thinking becomes an occult science that is honored by

many but practiced by few. Some tools of the old, forgotten ways are used for household decoration and arcane ceremonies – writing instruments, a pad of paper, and something called a "book" – but almost no one knows remember how they were used.

Freemasonry is currently somewhere in the middle of this hypothetical future quagmire. We have collapsed the degrees to increase lodge attendance for Master Masons' meetings and we have reduced the learning requirements to be a Master Mason. We are promoting ourselves by citing our pedigree, social opportunities, and the availability of *bling*.

That can keep us afloat for a few years. Then what?

Let me circle back to my original point. Early Freemasons saw our institution as one which could teach men to think. About what? The sciences, morality, religion, art, and even reality itself. Memorization requirements were not intended to keep men down. They were intended to *elevate* men.

I HOPE YOU'VE ENJOYED THIS BOOK. I WELCOME FEEDBACK and comments. If you've found this book valuable, or at least interesting, please share it with others.

Godspeed to all traveling men.

FINALE

"For the fabric of this universe is like a labyrinth to the contemplative mind, where doubtful paths, deceitful imitations of things and their signs, winding and intricate folds and knots of nature everywhere present themselves, and a way must constantly be made through the forests of experience and particular natures, with the aid of the uncertain light of the senses, shining and disappearing by fits. But the guides who offer their services are (as has been said) themselves confused, and increase the number of wanderings and of wanderers...

"We, for our part at least, overcome by the eternal love of truth, have committed ourselves to uncertain, steep, and desert tracks, and trusting and relying on Divine assistance, have borne up our mind against the violence of opinions, drawn up as it were in battle array, against our own internal doubts and scruples, against the mists and clouds of nature, and against fancies flitting on all sides around us: that we might at length collect some more trustworthy and certain indications for the living and posterity."

- Sir Francis Bacon, *The Great Instauration*

FINALE

An illustration from Robert Fludd's "Tomas secundus de supernaturali, naturali, praeternaturali et contranaturali microcosmi historia." The rungs of this ladder are labeled, from bottom to top: Sense, Imagination, Reason, Understanding, Intelligence, The Word.

APPENDIX 1: MEMORY OBJECT SAMPLES

These are only examples. Whenever possible, create your own Memory Objects. The ones you create will be more memorable than the objects created for you.

- Abide - a bride
- About - a boxer (boxing bout), a trout
- Accord - accordion, a cord
- Act - axe
- Admission - movie ticket stub
- Admit - mitten with + (addition sign) on it
- After - raptor
- Agreeable - a gerbil
- Aid - first aid kit
- All - awl, shawl
- Allusion - illusion (magician)
- And - rubber band, hand, band instrument
- And be - Aunt Bee

APPENDIX 1: MEMORY OBJECT SAMPLES

- Answer - Q & A, ants, Anwar, green phone icon
- Any - Annie
- Apply - plywood, apple, apple with eye
- Approach - A broach, a roach
- Are - R
- Arrange - A gun range target
- As - ass
- Aside - acid
- At - bat
- Beautiful - butterfly
- Because - big claws
- Before - beef ore
- Brethren - bread hen
- But - bud
- By - bye (a waving hand)
- Chamber - chamber pot
- Cheat - cheetah, Cheetos
- Chiliad - chili ad
- Class - glass
- Cold - snowflake, ice
- Con... - convict in a striped outfit
- Conducted - conductor
- Confidence - convict "Fido" on a fence
- Confusion - Confucius
- Constituted - constitution
- Custom - costume
- Defraud - deep-fried (deep fryer)
- Degree - thermometer
- Distinct - dirty stinky Socks
- Distress - distressed wood
- Discord - guitar cord

APPENDIX 1: MEMORY OBJECT SAMPLES

- Due - library card, Mountain Dew
- East - box of yeast, Empire State Building
- Emblem - M blooming, imbecile
- Envy - ivy
- Errantry - swaying tree
- Evasion - Cajun Eve
- Even - oven, Eve
- Entitled - book with "N" as the title
- Equivocation - equal nation
- Fane - plane
- Far - fur, binoculars, fire
- Finally - shark's fin
- Form - foam
- Found - pound
- Fraternity - Greek frat symbols
- Free Will - "Free Willy" orca
- From - rum
- Further - feather
- Furthermore - feather Thor
- Gain - Gain detergent
- Gloomy - glue, gooey
- Great - grape (purple)
- Grip - grit (John Wayne in True Grit)
- Have - ½ or a cleaver
- Has that - hazmat
- Heretofore - Harrison Ford, two hares in a Ford
- Him - hymn
- His - snake hissing, restroom "male" sign
- Holy - halo
- How were - Howard
- I - eye

APPENDIX 1: MEMORY OBJECT SAMPLES

- I am – IAMS dog food
- I was – iris, eye-wash station
- If – F
- In – inn or N
- Inculcate – Calculate (calculator)
- Incunabulum – Incan album
- In which – sandwich
- Interrupt – enter up
- Into – A bottle of Nitrogen (N2)
- Initiation – any initiation device
- Is – snake hissing, fizz, Isis
- Is it – biscuit
- It – mitt (glove) or person
- Jr Warden – JaWS
- Just – jester
- Justice – Lady Justice (Blind Justice) statue
- Justly – Justice Lee
- Keep – key shaped like P
- Knock – door knocker
- Law, Laws, Lawfully – police badge
- Let us – lettuce
- Length – link (sausage link)
- Like – thumbs up, spike
- Lodge – log
- Manner – manor
- Masonry – mason jar
- Masque – mask
- May – Mayflower, Mae West, emerald (birthstone)
- Me – meat
- Mental – dental
- Middle – griddle with bacon strips forming "M"

APPENDIX 1: MEMORY OBJECT SAMPLES

- Mind - mime, a brain
- Morality - shoulder angel
- Most - moist cake mix, toast with burned M
- Must - rust, a mast
- My - Mai-tai
- Nature - Mother Nature
- Necessary - nest of a canary
- Neither - knee hair
- Noble - nobleman
- North - Norse
- Nor - oar with N on paddle, north on compass
- Not - Knot
- Obey - Obi Wan
- Obligation - oblong gate, with a chain on it
- Of - UV sunblock, oven
- Or - oar
- Ordered - waitress
- Orion - Oreo cookie
- Orus - orafice
- Other - otter
- Ought - noose (knot above rope shaped like 'O')
- Our - flour, hourglass
- Pass - a press or backstage pass on a lanyard
- Peace - peace sign
- Penalty - yellow flag
- Pervade - Darth Vader
- Performance - dancing cat
- Philolaus - pillow mouse
- Pillar - pillow, pill
- Poor - pockets turned out, broken piggy bank
- Portal - port hole

APPENDIX 1: MEMORY OBJECT SAMPLES

- Practice - lattice in shape of a P
- Prepare - Preparation H
- Presence - presents (wrapped gifts)
- Principal - principle, prince
- Profession - professor holding a bun
- Promise - Promise butter
- Proceeding - pro (golfer) seeding
- Prudence - prune juice
- Regulations - RAGU rations, regulator
- Repeat - repeater rifle
- Represent - dinged up present newly wrapped (re-presented)
- Repudiate - Rasputin eating a date
- Rest - nest
- Rule(s) - ruler(s)
- See that - CPAP mask
- Sr Warden - SaW
- Sent - tent, sin, cement
- Serves - serving tray
- Shall - shell, shawl
- Should - wooden shield
- Show - shoe, snow, snow shoe
- Sincere - Zen sphere
- So - sewing machine, thread, sewing needle
- So shall - seashell
- Solemn - salami
- South - Confederate flag
- Stage - stooge
- Stand - podium
- Steadfast - breakfast
- Suffer - surfboard

APPENDIX 1: MEMORY OBJECT SAMPLES

- Swear - @!$%
- Symbols - musical symbols
- Taught - tater tot
- Teach - torch
- Than - van
- That - hat
- The - golf tee, tea bag
- The least - tea leaves, yeast
- Thence - fence
- There - pointed finger, bear
- These - keys
- They - hay
- This - thighs
- To - two
- To all - Total cereal (To-al)
- To the - toothy (a wide smile)
- To them - totem
- Too - two
- Took - hook
- Trial - judge in robes/wig
- Tranquility - Trans-Am on a quilt
- Unfeifned - un-fanged (toothless vampire)
- Universal - unicycle
- Until - sundial
- Unto - UNO playing card "2"
- Upon - apron, coupon
- Us - bus, map of U.S.
- Violate - violet
- Virtue - virtual shoe
- Was - fuzz
- Was said - salad

APPENDIX 1: MEMORY OBJECT SAMPLES

- Watchful - watch
- We - "wee" Leprechaun
- Were - whirring, a werewolf
- West - cowboy, a cactus
- What - wok, white wok
- Whatsoever - wok atop a sewing lever
- When - hen
- Where - chair with W shaped back
- Which - witch
- While - wale
- Will be - Willoughby, will—o-wisp and bee
- Who - owl
- Why - whey
- With - width (measuring tape)
- Without - white-out
- Wold - mold
- Worshipful Master - Worcestershire baster
- Yet - Yeti
- Wrong - red "x", "Wrong Way" sign
- You - U-turn sign, inverted horseshoe
- Youth - tooth or YMCA "Y" symbol
- ...ful - full (gas tank)
- ...ing - king
- ...ly - General Lee, Bruce Lee

APPENDIX 2: ARCHAIC WORDS EXPLAINED

There are a lot of archaic and difficult words in our craft. It's important that you take the time to learn the meanings of any words you don't understand before trying to memorize them. Below I've listed a few of the more difficult ones, in addition to their definitions. I'm not, however, an "authority" in the field archaic Masonic terminology. If my definition doesn't seem quite right or appropriate, look it up online or ask a brother for help.

Also, the definitions I've provided assume the words appear in a Masonic context. For example, an "alarm" within our ritual is typically a knock or series of knocks on a door, while outside of Freemasonry the word has a much broader meaning.

- About: around
- Accord: harmonious agreement, a decision that does not conflict with a person's conscience

APPENDIX 2: ARCHAIC WORDS EXPLAINED

- Accordingly: appropriately, in the correct manner
- Appellation: title or name
- Alarm: knock, or series of knocks
- Allude: refer to something indirectly, i.e., without actually using its name
- Arise: stand up
- Attend: take responsibility for, respond to
- Before (as a location): in front of
- Bind: attach two things or concepts to each other
- Cause (as a verb): ensure that a required action is performed
- Caused: required to do something
- Charge (as a noun): a demand or requirement
- Charge (as a verb): to demand or require something
- Circumscribe: keep something within certain limits, stay within boundaries
- Clothe (a verb): usually "arrange the apron" Compose: bring together individuals to form a group (lodge)
- Conduct: lead or escort a person, usually a candidate
- Conducted: led, escorted
- Constituted: assembled
- Dedicated: done in honor of someone
- Demand (verb): request a required action to be performed
- Design: 1. purpose or intention; 2: blueprint, plan
- Desirous (of): wants
- Destitute: very poor
- Dispose: 1. place someone at a certain location; 2. share with someone else

APPENDIX 2: ARCHAIC WORDS EXPLAINED

- Distinct: unmistakable and clearly distinguishable from all others like it
- Discover: see
- Divest: take away, remove
- Due: correct
- Duly: correctly
- Effluvia: unpleasant smells or scents
- Emblematic: symbolic, represents something else
- Endowed: in possession of, or more simply, "has"
- Engagements: activities that occur at a fixed time and place
- Equivocation: ignoring the plain meaning of a statement by using a creative interpretation
- Erected: built, constructed
- Evasion: avoiding a commitment
- Exalted: noble, superior, elevated
- Examination: questioning
- Form: a pose, specific placement of arms and legs
- Free will (of): voluntarily
- Further: additional
- Gain: obtain, be granted
- Garments: usually, but not always, the clothes worn by a candidate for degrees
- Hele: keep secret
- Hereby: in this way, in this manner
- Hereon: on this basis, from this point forward
- Hoodwink: blindfold
- Impart: communicate, repeat
- Instruction: direction to do something
- Instrument: tool
- Invoke: call upon for assistance

APPENDIX 2: ARCHAIC WORDS EXPLAINED

- Irrevocable: permanent
- Just: fair-minded, impartial
- Laid aside: temporarily or conveniently ignored
- Liberal: free, unrestrained
- Meridian: highest point (the sun is at its meridian at noon)
- Metals: metal objects
- Mote: may, must
- Movable: capable of being removed
- Nay: no
- Open: officially begin
- Ought: should
- Pass: move from one condition, position or location to another
- Passion: emotion
- Peculiar: special or unique
- Penalty: the consequence or result of a (usually forbidden) action
- Place (as a noun): in lodge, a location which is left or right of a Master or the Warden
- Place (as a verb): put in a certain location
- Portion: share or piece of something larger, equally divided and distributed
- Presume: 1. dare or unwisely decide to do something that is prohibited; 2. assume
- Propound: verbally present or communicate
- Recapitulation: summary, the main points
- Recollection: memory, remembrance
- Reconducted: returned (escorted) to a previous location
- Rectitude: righteousness, goodness

APPENDIX 2: ARCHAIC WORDS EXPLAINED

- Regular: normal, as would be expected
- Reinvest: return to someone something that was taken at an earlier point in time
- Repass: re-enter
- Repudiate: deny or refuse to meet an obligation
- Reservation: a concern or the inability to accept something as true
- Retire: go to a place outside of the lodge room
- Solemn: serious, dignified
- Speculative: theoretical, academic, abstract
- Station: assigned position of Officers in the East, West, or South
- Steadfast: never changing, permanent, constant
- Subdue: control or manage
- Sublime: beautiful and inspirational
- Such (a manner): like this, in this way
- Taper: a thin candle
- Taken: presumed to be
- Thereby: as a result of something just mentioned
- Therefor: in return for something given, which was just mentioned
- Thereof: a reference back to something just mentioned
- Thereon: on top of something just mentioned
- Thus: in this way, as a result of
- Ties: links, connections
- Toilsome: difficult and tiring
- Token: symbol of something, evidence of something
- Transgress: overstep your limits, break a law or rule
- Tried: tested, quizzed, interrogated

- Truly: verifiably, genuinely
- Tyle: to guard
- Tyled: guarded
- Undertaking: activity, task
- Votaries: advocates, devoted members
- Well-founded: something with a good, solid, and proper foundation
- Whence: where
- Whereby: as a result of, brought about by
- Whither: to what place?
- Withdraw: quit, leave
- Without (as a location): outside of
- Wittingly: intentionally
- Worshipful: honored, respected

APPENDIX 3: NOTATIONS

Lectures can be difficult to memorize because of their length. But lines associated with roles (in which you must do or say something and then wait for other brothers to speak or act before saying or doing something else) can be equally daunting.

Though lecturers typically have many more words to memorize than a brother who needs to memorize only those lines associated with one role, lecturers proceed from start to finish without interruption and without the hazard of waiting for a cue from another brother which may never come, or which may come in the wrong form.

Additionally, lecturers have few if any actions to perform as they speak. Though they may make an occasional gesture with their hands or head, they spend the majority of their time planted in just one location. This physically idle state allows lecturers to focus on their words with few distractions.

Masons memorizing interactive roles don't have this

APPENDIX 3: NOTATIONS

luxury. They are like actors in a play. Though their lines may be shorter and fewer in number than those of a lecturer, their lines are discontinuous. A lecturer can "cruise" through his lecture while a Mason playing a role must recite his lines, or perform his actions, then wait, often for a very long time, before being cued to again speak or act. This means that, in addition to memorizing his lines and actions, a non-lecturer also needs to memorize the physical and verbal cues of others.

If you are memorizing a role instead of a lecture, you may find it helpful make little notations in your cipher or monitor that can help you characterize the actions and words of other participants. As your studies of Masonic rituals advance, you'll observe that there is particular rhythm to, for example, the degrees. Knowing this rhythm is a great help in the memorization process, and notations are one method for recognizing those rhythms.

On the following pages I've included symbols that can be used as notations, though you're of course free to develop your own. These notations are best made in the outer margins adjacent to pertinent lines or actions.

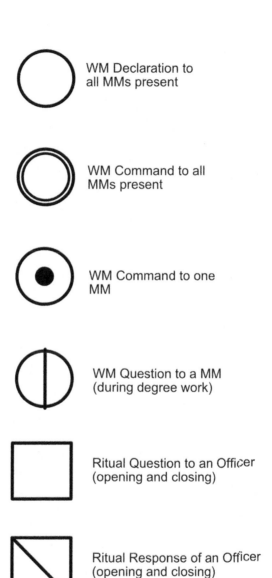

Challenge

 Response to Challenge

 Candidate Directed or Questioned

 Candidate Response

 Obligation cited

 Obligation repeated

Explanation/Insight

 Ritual Action

 Announcement or Pronouncement by Deacon

 Permission Given

 Education/History/Lecture

ALSO BY BOB W. LINGERFELT

The Travels of Gaius: A Masonic Tale of Allusions

The Travels of Gaius is an entertaining but instructional tale intended to familiarize new Freemasons with fundamental Masonic concepts. It is the story of an adventurous young man named Gaius who travels to a strange, unknown land in his search for a thing of great value that was lost long ago. Aided by Dux, an enigmatic guide from a mysterious Order, our hero finds himself tested by the powerful Wardens of the Gates and the ingeniously wicked creatures that lurk in the realms of Beauty, Strength, Wisdom, and Ignorance.

The story's scenes and characters are designed to give a new initiate a basic but holistic comprehension of certain elementary Masonic subjects. These include, among other things, the nature of the three pillars; the cardinal points of the lodge; the roles, locations, and jewels of the lodge officers; the lesser and greater lights; the four cardinal virtues; circumambulation; the movement of the sun; the Mosaic pavement; and the importance of Deity.

These diverse topics have been woven together in such a way that they can be easily understood and associated with little or no conscious effort on the part of the Masonic reader. Though this book's target reader is the newly obligated brother of any degree, even the established Freemasons might discover a few ideas worthy of contemplation.

Made in the USA
Middletown, DE
03 January 2023

19456159R00126